THE NEW ECONOMICS

THE NEW ECONOMICS

FOR INDUSTRY, GOVERNMENT, EDUCATION

Second Edition

W. Edwards Deming

Massachusetts Institute of Technology
Center for Advanced Engineering Study

Published by the Massachusetts Institute of Technology
Center for Advanced Engineering Study
Cambridge, MA 02139

Printed in the United States of America

Second Printing, October 1995

International Standard Book Number: 0-911379-07-X

Library of Congress Catalog Card Number: 94-79284

Contents

Description of Figures   *page*   v

Foreword   ix

Notes to the Second Edition   xi

About the Author   xiii

Preface   xv

1.   How Are We Doing?   1

2.   The Heavy Losses   22

3.   Introduction to a System   49

4.   A System of Profound Knowledge   92

5.   Leadership   116

6.   Management of People   121

7.   The Red Beads   154

8.   Shewhart and Control Charts   172

9.   The Funnel   190

10.   Some Lessons in Variation   207

Appendix: Continuing Purchase
of Supplies and Services   227

Index   235

Description of Figures

Figure   *Page*

1. Elimination of defects does not guarantee jobs in the future. Something other than zero defects is required.   11

2. Management improve style and performance. The product enjoys a better market; the number of jobs increases.   13

3. Flow diagram of the steps taken at the Sacred Heart League to solicit donations.   19

4. Figure 3 redrawn as a deployment flow chart.   21

5. A numerical goal that lies beyond the upper control limit will not be achieved by the present process.   42

6. Production viewed as a system.   58

7. Figure 6 broken into competitive segments. The system is destroyed.   66

8. Some possible distributions of time of delivery.   80

9. Interdependence, from low to high.   97

10. The forces of destruction that come from the present style of reward, and their effects.   122

Figure	*Description*	*Page*
11.	The decline that we attribute to the present style of management, and the improvement once transformation is accomplished.	124
12.	A system of people, before and after improvement.	127
13.	The Plan-Do-Study-Act Cycle (Shewhart Cycle): A flow diagram for learning and for improvement of a product or process.	132
14.	Stages proposed in the development of a new engine.	134
15.	Recommended concentration of cost and effort, in the early stages, in the development of a process or product.	138
16.	Payroll time card. Too many signatures, and too much arithmetic required of the employee.	141
17.	Beads and paddle.	155
18.	Posters to help the Willing Workers.	159
19.	The experiment with the Red Beads: Data, calculation of control limits, display and interpretation of the control chart.	160
20.	Distribution of Red Beads in 53 experiments.	166
21.	Flow diagram for use of a control chart.	183

Figure	Description	Page
32.	Chart for the U.S. trade deficit over a 27-month period shows a stable system of ups and downs.	215
33.	Example of a simple loss function; a parabola with minimum loss at the bottom of the curve.	217
34.	Example of use of a loss function generated by a gadget on and off that holds parts within specifications.	220
35.	Example of a discontinuous loss function.	221
36.	Example of a loss function for failure to meet a deadline, such as to catch a train.	222
37.	Example of use of a loss function to show the importance of shrinkage at the nominal value.	225

Figure	Description	Page
22.	Plot of the number of fires per month in a business establishment.	187
23.	Record of drops of the marble through the funnel under Rule 1.	191
24.	Record of drops of the marble through the funnel under Rule 2.	192
25.	Record of drops of the marble through the funnel under Rule 3.	193
26.	Record of drops of the marble through the funnel under Rule 4.	194
27.	Four charts of the rules of the funnel by use of data from the experiment with the Red Beads.	206
28.	Chart to show, day by day, the time of arrival of a school bus (by Patrick Nolan, age 11).	209
29.	Control chart for actual costs on 20 projects shows natural deviation of 21 per cent above and below estimated costs.	211
30.	Control charts for accuracy of inventory, before and after improvement of accuracy.	212
31.	Sales in percentage achieved by eight salesmen from two product lines.	214

Foreword

The wisdom and lessons of W. Edwards Deming live on. Our father continued to make changes to the manuscript for this second edition of *The New Economics for Industry, Government, Education* until his death in December 1993. The revisions were intended to provide further clarification and were often based directly on comments from readers of the first edition. He remained sharply focused on helping people gain the knowledge necessary for transformation to a new style of management. The route to transformation is to apply the System of Profound Knowledge outlined in this book.

Our father found joy in work and joy in learning throughout his long and productive life. As he wrote in *The New Economics,* "Anyone that enjoys his work is a pleasure to work with." We know from our interactions with people all over the world that W. Edwards Deming helped others to find joy in their endeavors and that his work touched them at the deepest levels.

In November 1993 our father established the W. Edwards Deming Institute. The aim of the Institute is to foster understanding of The Deming System of Profound Knowledge to advance commerce, prosperity, and peace. With the help and efforts of those committed to this aim, we strive to carry on his legacy.

Diana Deming Cahill

Linda Deming Ratcliff

Notes to the Second Edition

Until his death in December 1993, Dr. Deming was at work on revisions to *The New Economics.* This second edition reflects Dr. Deming's changes. For the most part, the changes were in Chapter Four, where he wished to reinforce the point that the System of Profound Knowledge comprises an outside view essential to the management of a system.

An appendix has been added to the second edition, titled "Continuing Purchase of Supplies and Service." Dr. Deming included this material in his Four Day Seminars. This addition will be helpful to readers who wish to better understand his writings on relationships with suppliers.

Dr. Deming refers to his earlier text, *Out of the Crisis*[1], many times in *The New Economics.* The reader who wishes to gain a deeper understanding of Dr. Deming's ideas should study *Out of the Crisis.* For a closer look at Dr. Deming's life, and to find a list of his publications, the reader may refer to the text *The World of W. Edwards Deming*[2], authored by Cecelia Kilian, his secretary of thirty-nine years.

[1]W. Edwards Deming (Massachusetts Institute of Technology, Center for Advanced Engineering Study, 1986).

[2]Cecelia S. Kilian (SPC Press, 1992).

Preface

This book is for people who are living under the tyranny of the prevailing style of management. The huge, long-range losses caused by this style of management have led us into decline. Most people imagine that the present style of management has always existed, and is a fixture. Actually, it is a modern invention—a prison created by the way in which people interact. This interaction afflicts all aspects of our lives—government, industry, education, healthcare.

We have grown up in a climate of competition between people, teams, departments, divisions, pupils, schools, universities. We have been taught by economists that competition will solve our problems. Actually, competition, we see now, is destructive. It would be better if everyone would work together as a system, with the aim for everybody to win. What we need is cooperation and transformation to a new style of management.

The route to transformation is what I call *Profound Knowledge*. The system of profound knowledge is composed of four parts, all related to each other:

Appreciation for a system
Knowledge about variation
Theory of knowledge
Psychology

The aim of this book is to start the reader on the road to knowledge, and to create a yearning for more knowledge.

My 14 Points for Management (*Out of the Crisis,* MIT/CAES, 1986) follow naturally as application of the system of profound knowledge, for transformation from the present style of management to one of optimization.

This is also a textbook for students of engineering, economics, and business. The purpose of a school of business should not be to perpetuate the present style of management, but to transform it. Students of engineering may learn the new tools and theories of engineering, but their successful application requires new methods of management. In other words, the purpose of a school should be to prepare students for the future, not for the past.

The first two chapters describe the prevailing style of management, with suggestions for better practice. Chapter 3 describes the theory of a system. In an optimized system, everybody benefits—stockholders, suppliers, employees, and customers. Chapter 4 introduces the system of profound knowledge, which provides a lens through which to understand and optimize the organizations that we work in. Later chapters expand the theories of Chapters 3 and 4—with examples and applications to business, education, and government.

Many people have made contributions to the preparation of this book. Notes of appreciation appear throughout. It is a pleasure to record here the outstanding devotion of my secretary, Cecelia S. Kilian.

THE NEW
ECONOMICS

1

How Are We Doing?

Nothing can do you so much harm as a lousy competitor.
Be thankful for a good competitor.—Alfred Politz.

A new world: Information flows. The people of the world no longer live in isolation. Information flows across borders. Movies, TV, VCR, and FAX tell us instantly about other people, how they live, what they enjoy. People make comparisons. Anybody wishes to live like somebody else. Anybody else lives better, so everybody supposes.

How may people live as other people live? People blame their plight on to the government and its leaders, or to management and its leaders. They may be correct. But will change in leadership assure better living? What if the new leaders are no better? How could they be? How much time have new leaders to demonstrate that they have brought a better life? In other words, how patient are people? What are the criteria that people use for judgment?

By what method could new leaders bring improvement in living? Do they possess knowledge requisite for improvement? What characteristics ought a leader to possess? Will best efforts bring improvement? Unfortunately, no. Best efforts and hard work, not guided by new knowledge, they only dig deeper the pit that we are in. The aim of this book is to provide new knowledge.

Knowledge necessary for improvement comes from outside.

This book will teach and explore some basic ground rules of knowledge for change. There is no substitute for knowledge.

Necessity for trade. In order to improve living in a material way as well as in a spiritual way, people must trade goods and services with other people. Trade is a two-way street. For a community to import anything, it must export something in payment.

The market is the world. Today, the market for almost any product may be anywhere in this world. Likewise, supplies may come from almost anywhere. Here in my hand is a tiny clock. Inscribed on it are these words:

Assembled in China with
Swiss parts made in Hong Kong.

The pen that I am using bears the brand of a German company, Faber-Castell, famous for office supplies. Looking at it carefully one day, I discovered that it was made in Japan.

What is quality? The basic problem anywhere is quality. What is quality? A product or a service possesses quality if it helps somebody and enjoys a good and sustainable market. Trade depends on quality.

Have we been living on fat? Some countries live in part by export of nonrenewable materials such as oil, coal, iron

2

ore, copper, aluminum, scrap metal. These are temporary blessings: they can not last forever. To live on gifts, credit, or borrowed money is not a long-term solution, either.

In the year 1920, iron ore dug from the Mesabi Range (northwest of Duluth) yielded 74 per cent iron. Today, the yield is 33 per cent, so low that steel companies concentrate the iron right at the mine into iron pellets 74 per cent iron, to save cost in transportation by rail to the docks at Duluth, and onward by boat to Cleveland. There is still a lot of iron in the Mesabi Range, 50 million tons of pellets per year, but the cream is gone. Forests may disappear. One of our best exports in terms of inflow of dollars is scrap metal, nonrenewable.

We ship out, for dollars, iron ore, partially refined, aluminum, nickel, copper, coal, all nonrenewable.

We have been wasting our natural resources, and worse, as we shall see, destroying our people.

How does the United States stand? How is the United States doing in respect to balance of trade? The answer is that we are not doing well.

North America has contributed much to new knowledge and to applications of knowledge. In the year 1910, the United States made half the manufactured product of the world. The United States, by efficient production and natural resources, beginning around 1920 and for decades, put manufactured products in the hands of millions of people the world over that could not otherwise have had them. Our quality was good enough to create appetite for more.

3

A further advantage came to North America for a decade after World War II. North America was the only part of the world that could produce at full capacity manufactured goods. The rest of the industrial world lay in ruins from the war. The rest of the world were our customers, willing buyers for whatever North America could produce. Gold flowed into Fort Knox.

One of our best exports, one that brings in dollars, is materials for war. We could greatly expand this income but for moral reasons. American aircraft have about 70 per cent of the world market, and bring in huge amounts of dollars. Another important export is scrap metal. We can't use it, so we sell it. The Japanese paid us about 18 cents for the metal in the microphone that I use in lectures. We buy the metal back from them in the form of a microphone for $2000, possibly $1800—value added! Scrap cardboard and paper bring in dollars. Chemicals are doing well, pharmaceuticals also. Timber brings in dollars. Timber is renewable. Scrap cardboard and paper are renewable. Equipment for construction is an important export, so I understand. American movies, a service industry, bring in dollars. Banking and insurance were at one time important, almost competitive with British banking and insurance, but no longer. The biggest U.S. bank is today far down the list of the biggest banks in the world.

What happened? Everyone expected the good times to continue and to wax better and better. It is easy to manage a business in an expanding market, and easy to suppose that economic conditions can only grow better and better.

4

In contrast with expectations, we find, on looking back, that we have been on an economic decline for three decades. It is easy to date an earthquake, but not a decline.

Around 1955, Japanese goods started to flow in. The price was good, and the quality was good, not like the shoddy quality that came from Japan before the war and just after, cheap but worth the price. Preference for imported items—some at least—gradually climbed and became a threat to North American industry.

It is hard to believe that anything is different now than in 1950. The change has been gradual, not visible week to week. We can only see the decline by looking back. A cat is unaware that dusk has settled upon the earth. Her pupils expand as light recedes, but she is as helpless as any of us in total darkness.

Some industries are doing better than ever. There are more automobiles in the United States than ever before, and more travel by air. Do such figures mean decline or advance? An answer should take into account that in 1958 we had intercity trains. There was a choice, air or train. Now, we have only limited train service; the only choice is to go by air or by automobile.

There was until a few years ago a favorable balance of trade in agricultural products—wheat, cotton, soybeans, to name a few—but no longer. Imports of agricultural products have overtaken exports, and as someone in one of my seminars pointed out, if we had the figures to put illicit drugs into the accounting, our deficit in agricultural products would show up worse than the published figures.

5

What must we do? We in North America may accept the fact that we no longer excel in the manufacture of low-cost items in great volume. This business has gone to automation, Mexico, Taiwan, Korea, and elsewhere. We can elevate our economy with specialized services and products. This change will require knowledge. In other words, our problem is education and development of a culture that puts value on learning.

How may we improve education? The reader will be aware that improvement of education, and the management of education, require application of the same principles that must be used for the improvement of any process, manufacturing or service. Innovation and improvement of education will require leaders (see Ch. 5).

What state of company is in the best position to improve? A man in one of my seminars arose with the question, "Where is the crisis? We and our competitors in the United States have 70 per cent of the world's market for aeroplanes." My answer was that a company that is healthy, doing well, is in an excellent position to improve management, product, and service, thus to contribute to the economic welfare of itself and to the rest of us, and moreover has the greatest obligation to improve. A monopoly is in fact in the best possible position to improve year by year, and has the greatest obligation to do so. A company that is on the rocks can only think of survival—short-term.

The customer's expectations. There is much talk about the customer's expectations. Meet the customer's expectations. The fact is that the customer expects only what you and your competitor have led him to expect. He is a rapid learner.

Does the customer invent new product or service? The customer generates nothing. No customer asked for electric lights. There was gas and gas mantles, which gave good light. The first electric lights had carbon filaments. They were fragile and inefficient. No customer asked for photography. No customer asked for the telegraph, nor for a telephone. No customer asked for an automobile. We have horses: what could be better? No customer asked for pneumatic tires. Tires are made of rubber. It is silly to think of riding on air. The first pneumatic tires in the United States were not good. The user had to carry with him rubber cement, plugs, and a pump, and know how to use them. I can testify to that. No customer asked for an integrated circuit. No customer asked for a pocket-radio. No customer asked for facsimile.

An educated customer may have a firm idea about his needs, what he would wish to purchase. He may be able to specify these needs so that a supplier may understand them. A wise customer will nevertheless listen and learn from suggestions from a supplier. They should work together as a system, not as one trying to outdo the other. This is Point 4 of the 14 points, in the book *Out of the Crisis*.[1] We learn

[1]W. Edwards Deming (Massachusetts Institute of Technology, Center for Advanced Engineering Study, 1986).

7

more about this relationship in Chapter 3.

People are asking for better schools, with no clear idea how to improve education, nor even how to define improvement of education.

Is it sufficient to have happy customers? loyal customers? The customer expects only what the producer has led him to expect. He is a rapid learner; compares one product with another, one source with another. We certainly do not wish to have an unhappy customer, but it will not suffice to have customers that are merely satisfied. A satisfied customer may switch. Why not? He might come out better for the switch.

It is good to have loyal customers, the customer that comes back, waits in line, and brings a friend with him. This could all be true, but it will not suffice to have loyal customers.

It is the same for service. The customer takes what he gets (laundry, mail, transportation). He invents nothing. But again, he is a rapid learner. When Federal Express and competitors offer overnight service at many times the cost of postage, the customer runs for the new service. He forgets or does not even know that in other parts of the industrial world, a postage stamp would provide overnight service.

No customer asked for a pacemaker. No customer asked for a battery in his pacemaker that will last 10 years, and which holds in storage information on the speed and regularity of heartbeats over the past month.

Innovation. It is good to introduce, by innovation, a new product that will do the job better. But where does innovation come from?

Where today are the makers of carburetors? There was a time when every automobile had a carburetor, at least one. How could an automobile run without a carburetor? The makers of carburetors improved their product year by year. Customers were happy, loyal.

What happened? Innovation. Came the fuel injector, which does the job of a carburetor, and a lot more. The fuel injector costs more than a carburetor, but when one line of cars adopted it, all the others followed. Carburetors went out, even on trucks. Fewer readers, year by year, will remember carburetors.

In time, the fuel injector will be displaced. New ways to inject fuel and air into the combustion chamber, and a new type of engine, will come forth and render obsolete the fuel injector.

Few people will remember vacuum tubes. There was a time when a radio depended on vacuum tubes. An eight-tube radio occupied space. A nine-tube radio was better than an eight-tube radio, but occupied more space. Makers of vacuum tubes improved year by year the power of vacuum tubes, and made them smaller and smaller. Customers were happy, loyal. Came along, however, the work of William Shockley and others in the Bell Telephone Laboratories on the diode and transistor effect, which led to the integrated circuit. Happy customers of vacuum tubes deserted vacuum tubes and ran for the pocket-radio.

The moral is that it is necessary to innovate, to predict needs of the customer, give him more. He that innovates and is lucky will take the market.

What business are we in? The foregoing paragraphs might be subsumed under the question, "What business are we in?" In the case of carburetors, was it to make carburetors? Yes. The makers of carburetors made good carburetors, better and better. They were in the business of making carburetors. It would have been better had they been in business to put a stoichiometric mixture of fuel and air into the combustion chamber, and to invent something that would do it better than a carburetor. Innovation on the part of somebody else led to the fuel injector and to hard times for the makers of carburetors.

A good question for anybody in business to ask is *What business are we in?* To do well what we are doing—i.e., to turn out a good product, or good service, whatever it be? Yes, of course, but this is not enough. We must keep asking *What product or service would help our customers more?* We must think about the future. What will we be making 5 years from now? 10 years from now?[2]

No defects, no jobs. Absence of defects does not necessarily build business, does not keep the plant open (Fig. 1). Something more is required. In the case of automobiles, for

[2]The substance of this paragraph comes from contributions of Dr. Edward M. Baker.

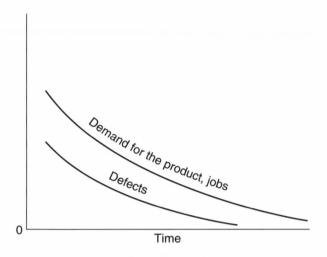

Fig. 1. Efforts on reduction of defects are successful. At the same time, the demand for product, sales, may slide downward toward zero. Simply to eliminate defects does not guarantee jobs in the future. No defects, no jobs, can go together. Something other than zero defects is required.

example, the customer—the one that keeps the plant open and running—may be interested in performance. He might include under performance not just acceleration but also behavior on ice, how the car steers at high speed, how it rides over bumps. Does it jump and skid on a rough road? How does the air conditioner work, and the heater?

The customer may also be interested in style—not just pictures of the automobile, but legibility of the numerous buttons and levers that the driver may try to read. Must I bend my neck almost to the breaking point to get into the car, or out? Comfort of passengers may be important.

Where will the passenger put his feet? his arms?

Performance and style, whatever these words mean in the minds of customers, must show constant improvement. Zero defects is not sufficient.

I listened all day, an unforgettable Thursday, to 10 presentations, reports of 10 teams, on reduction of defects. The audience was composed of 150 people, all working on reduction of defects, listening intently, with touching devotion to their jobs.

They did not understand, I think, that their efforts could in time be eminently successful—no defects—while their company declines. Something more must take place, for jobs (Fig. 2).

Their work is complicated. Some defects are related to each other. As one goes up, another goes down. An example of a family of problems, familiar to anyone in the automotive industry, is:

- Effort required to close the front door
- Noise from wind at high speed
- Rain

It is easy to use such a small amount of rubber around the edge of the door that it will be easy to close. But rain comes in, and the car at high speed is noisy from wind. It is easy to put in more rubber around the edge of the door to keep the rain out, and to diminish noise, but then only a strong man could close the door. Reduction of any one of the individual faults may lead to an intolerable level of one of the others. The problem is how to achieve a balance, a tolerable level for every one of the three.

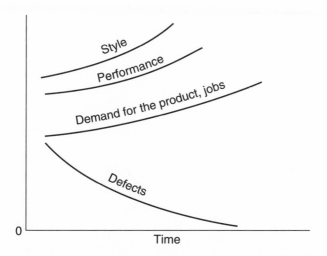

Fig. 2. Management improve style and performance of product. Efforts to eradicate defects are now effective. The product enjoys a better market; the number of jobs increases.

A look at some of the usual suggestions for improvement of quality. There is widespread interest in quality. Suppose that we were to conduct next Tuesday a national referendum with the question:

Are you in favor of improvement of quality?
Yes _____   No_____

The results would show, I believe, an avalanche in favor of quality. Moreover, unfortunately, almost everybody has the answer on how to achieve it. Just read letters to the editor, speeches, books. It seems so simple. Here are some of

13

the answers offered, all insufficient, some even negative in results:

Automation
New machinery
More computers
Gadgets
Hard work
Best efforts
Merit system; annual appraisal
Make everybody accountable
M.B.O. (management by objective, as practiced)
M.B.R. (management by results)
Rank people, rank teams, rank divisions, rank salesmen; reward them at the top, punish them at the bottom.
More SQC (statistical quality control)
More inspection
Establish an office of quality
Appoint someone as Vice President in Charge of Quality
Incentive pay
Work standards (quotas, time standards)
Zero defects
Meet specifications
Motivate people

What is wrong with these suggestions? The fallacies of the suggestions listed above will be obvious from subsequent pages of the text. Every one of them ducks the responsibility of management.

A company advertised that the future belongs to him that invests in it, and thereupon proceeded to invest heavily (40×10^9) in new machinery and automation. Results: trouble, overcapacity, high cost, low quality. It must be said in defense of the management that they obviously had faith in the future.

Is this amount enough to bleed a company to death? The interest on 40×10^9 at a mere 5 per cent per annum is 2×10^9. That is more than five million dollars per day, including Sundays and holidays, rain or shine. The investment, to be sensible, would have to show a profit far beyond 2×10^9 per year.

If the reader could follow me around in my consultations, he would perceive that much automation and much new machinery is a source of poor quality and high cost, helping to put us out of business. Much of it, if it performs as intended, is built for twice the capacity that is needed. Some of it is poorly designed, such as: make $\rightarrow$ inspect, make $\rightarrow$ inspect, make $\rightarrow$ inspect, ..., where inspection may not be economically the best procedure. (See Ch. 15 in *Out of the Crisis*.) Moreover, the apparatus for inspection usually gives more trouble than the apparatus for make.

The president of a company put quality into the hands of his plant managers. The results in time became obvious and embarrassing. Quality went down, as was predictable. A plant manager has no part in the design of the product. He is helpless. He can only try to do his job, meet his quota, conform to specifications, stamp out fires.

15

Of course we wish not to violate specifications, but to meet specifications is not enough. Zero defects is not enough, as we have seen. The pieces in an assembly must work together as a system.

The president of a company wrote in a journal:

> Our people in the plants are responsible for their own product and for its quality.

They are not. They can only try to do their jobs. The man that wrote the article, the president of the company, is the one that is responsible for quality.

The management of another company put the following dictum in the hands of all employees. It can only be described as pitiful.

> Our customers expect quality. The quality of our products is the primary responsibility of the operator in that he must make it correctly. The inspector shares this responsibility.

Again, the operator is not responsible for the product nor for its quality. He can only try to do his job. Moreover, responsibility divided between operator and inspector, as it is in the above quotation, assures mistakes and trouble. We shall learn more later about divided responsibility. The quality of the product is the responsibility of management, working with the customer.

The management in both of these examples handed their responsibilities over to people that are helpless to define quality and to innovate.

Another example: A group of consultants in management advertised thus:

> Computerized quality information systems provide the vital link between high technology and effective decision making.

I wish that management were as simple as that.

What is wrong with these declarations? Quality is determined by the top management. It can not be delegated. Moreover, an essential ingredient that I call profound knowledge is missing. There is no substitute for knowledge. Hard work, best efforts, and best intentions will not by themselves produce quality nor a market. Transformation of management is required—learning and application of profound knowledge. Chapter 4 shows an outline of profound knowledge.

Why did the plant close? I find amongst people in management and on the line deep concern about the future: Will there be jobs? In a number of sessions with the upper management of a large manufacturer, it turns out that they are under the supposition that if the hourly people would just put their backs to the job and do their work as they know how to do it, there would be jobs. I ask them, "Have you ever heard of a plant that closed? And why did it close? Shoddy workmanship?" No.

A plant was recognized as a model for efficiency, communication, good relationships with suppliers, written up

17

and filmed. The workmanship was superb. Why did the plant close? Answer: It was turning out a product that had lost the market. It is management's responsibility to look ahead, predict, change the product, keep the plant in operation.

Why did the bank close? Because of sluggishness at the tellers' windows, mistakes in bank statements, mistakes in calculation of interest on loans? Nonsense. All these operations could go off without blemish, while the bank closes. Who was responsible? The management, their bad loans.

Where is quality made? The answer is, by the top management. The quality of the output of a company can not be better than the quality determined at the top.

Job security and jobs are dependent on management's foresight to design product and service that will entice customers and build a market; to be ready, ahead of the customer, to modify product and service.

Example. One purpose of the Sacred Heart League, located near Memphis, is to provide medical care and food to impoverished, indigent children in four counties adjacent in the State of Mississippi. This purpose requires money. To get money, the League appeals to people on mailing lists. A flow diagram might look like Figure 3.

How would you measure the quality of this operation? An important measure would be the amount of money contributed, minus the cost of stages 0 to 7.

What does this measure of quality depend on?

18

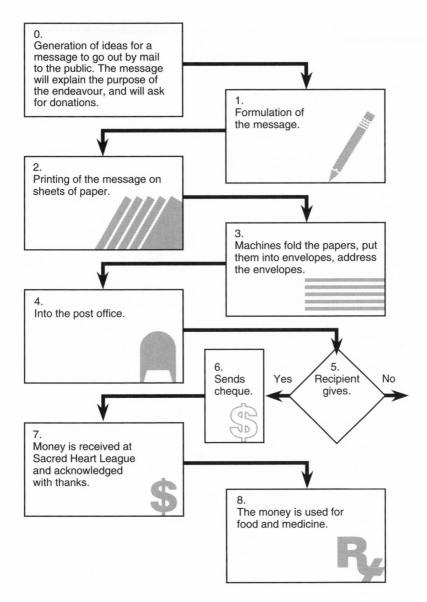

Fig. 3. Flow diagram of the steps taken at the Sacred Heart League to solicit donations.

Answer: the message in the envelopes. Whose responsibility is the message? Father Bob's, head of the Sacred Heart League.

The folding of the sheets of paper might go off perfectly. Likewise, the addresses on the envelopes might be flawless —every address an honest living human being. The postal system might do a perfect job of delivery, yet not enough money may come in to pay the cost. The Sacred Heart League would fold up. Receipts depend on the message. Flawless operations alone will not do it.

Another kind of quality would be how the League spends money received. Needs exceed receipts. This kind of quality can not be measured. We shall learn as we go on that the results of most activities of management can not be measured. For example, the benefit of training can not be measured. The cost we know: it shows on the ledger, but the benefits, no.

The flow diagram in Figure 3 shows the successive actions in the efforts of the Sacred Heart League. With a bit of training on flow diagrams, one could redraw Figure 3 as the deployment flow chart shown as Figure 4, for which I thank Dr. Myron Tribus.

Then why do we spend money for training? Answer: we believe that benefits in the future will far outweigh the cost. In other words, we manage by theory, prediction, not by figures.

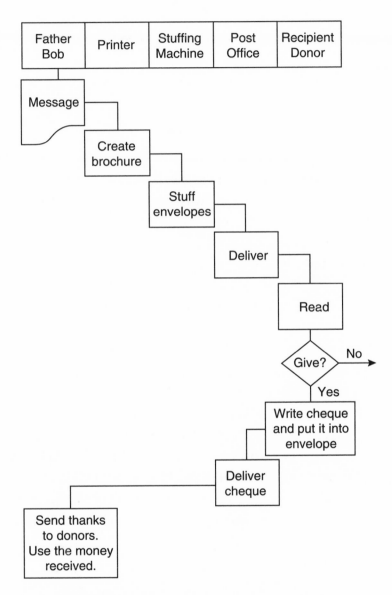

Fig. 4. This is Figure 3 redrawn by Dr. Myron Tribus as a deployment flow chart.

2

The Heavy Losses

I'd rather know a little less than to know so much that isn't
so.—Josh Billings.

Aim of this chapter. The present style of management is
the biggest producer of waste, causing huge losses whose
magnitudes can not be evaluated, can not be measured.
The aim of this chapter is to identify the most important
sources of loss (waste), and to offer suggestions for better
practice.

Unnecessary paperwork is a serious loss. A lot
of it originates in management's supposition that
the cure for repetition of a mistake or fraud is
more audit, more inspection. A letter to the *London Times,* 7 July 1990, displayed the fact that 23
per cent of the cost of running a hospital in the
United States goes for administration, against
only 5 per cent in the United Kingdom. Ask any
nurse in a hospital in the United States what duty
diminishes the effectiveness of her education and
aims—paperwork.

It is interesting to note that the prevailing system of management has been created by best efforts, without the
knowledge that we shall learn in later chapters.

We pause here to ask what is the effect of

    Hard work?

    Best efforts?

Answer: We thus only dig deeper the pit that we are in. Hard work and best efforts will not by themselves dig us out of the pit. In fact, it is only by illumination of outside knowledge that we may observe that we are in a pit.

The next chapter will be an attempt to provide a start on the knowledge that will help us to move out of the present system and into another.

We first show in detail some of the faulty practices of today.

SOME FAULTY PRACTICES OF MANAGEMENT, WITH SUGGESTIONS FOR BETTER PRACTICE

Present Practice Reactive: skills only required, not theory of management	Better Practice Theory of management required
Lack of constancy of purpose. **Short-term thinking. Emphasis on immediate results. Think in the present tense; no future tense.** **Keep up the price of the company's stock. Maintain dividends.** **Failure to optimize through time.** **Make this quarter look good. Ship everything on hand at the end of the month (or quarter). Never mind its quality; mark it shipped. Show it as accounts receivable.** **Defer till next quarter repairs, maintenance, and orders for material.**	**Adopt and publish constancy of purpose.** **Do some long-term planning.** **Ask this question: Where do we wish to be five years from now? Then, by what method?**

Quarterly reports required by the Federal Trade Commission and the Internal Revenue Service may be evil forces that require executives to keep an eye on the bottom line.

No number of successes in short-term problems will ensure long-term success.

Short-term solutions have long-term effects.

Of course, management must work on short-term problems as they turn up. But it is fatal to work exclusively on short-term problems, only stamping out fires.

Present Practice	Better Practice
Ranking people, salesmen, teams, divisions; reward at the top, punishment at the bottom. The so-called merit system.	Abolish ranking and the merit system. Manage the whole company as a system. The function of every component, every division, under good management, contributes toward optimization of the system.

Differences there will always be between any two people, any two salesmen, etc. The question is, what do the differences mean? Maybe nothing. Some knowledge about variation (statistical theory) is required to answer these questions.

Ranking is a farce. Apparent performance is actually attributable mostly to the system that the individual works in, not to the individual himself.

A simple equation will help to understand the futility of attempts to rank people. Let x be the contribution of some individual, (yx) the effect of the system on his performance. Then suppose that we have some number for his apparent performance, such as eight mistakes during the year, or sales of $8,000,000. Then

$$x + (yx) = 8$$

We need x. Unfortunately, there are two unknowns and only one equation. Johnny in the sixth grade knows that no one can solve this equation for x. Yet people that use the merit system think that they are solving it for x. They ignore the other term (yx), which is predominant.

There is another factor to take into account, the Pygmalion effect. Rated high at the start, anyone stays high. Rated low at the start, he stays low.[1]

Ranking creates competition between people, salesmen, teams, divisions. It demoralizes employees.

Ranking comes from failure to understand variation from common causes. (See *Out of the Crisis,* p. 310.)

The Red Beads (Ch. 7) will teach us some of the difficulties and errors in ranking people.

The so-called merit system introduces conflict between people. Emphasis goes to achievement of rank, merit, not on the work. The merit system destroys cooperation. We continue this theme in Chapter 6.

Raises in pay. Someone raised this question. How could you know whom to give raises in pay to if we don't have a merit system?

The answer is that the ranking of people is a farce. This we shall learn from the Red Beads in Chapter 7.

Whom to raise? Everybody within the system (see the top of page 118 in the book, *Out of the Crisis*). There will not be No. 1, No. 2, No. 3, No. last, as there will be no ranking. Anyone outside the control limits is in need of special help (Ch. 6).

---

[1]Robert Rosenthal and Lenore Jacobson, *Pygmalion in the Classroom* (Holt, Rinehart, and Winston, 1968).

The ranking of people indicates abdication of management.

The aim of anybody, under the merit system, is to please the boss. The result is destruction of morale. Quality suffers.

Judging people, putting them into slots, does not help them to do a better job.

What to do? Easy. Abolish next Monday morning the merit system in your company. Explain to your people your reasons why. They will rejoice and be glad.

Sadly, forced ranking of government employees is a mandate of Congress. Why does Congress tamper with activities that they know nothing about?

The day is here when anyone deprived of a raise in pay or of a job because of low rank may with justice file a grievance. He will win his case.

In the United States, the last ones to suffer are the people at the top. Dividends must not suffer.

In Japan, the pecking order is the opposite. A company in Japan that runs into economic hardship takes these steps:[2]

1. Cut the dividend. Maybe cut it out.

2. Reduce salaries and bonuses of top management.

3. Further reduction for top management.

4. Last of all, the rank and file are asked to help out. People that do not need to work may take a furlough. People that can take early retirement may do so, now.

5. Finally, if necessary, a cut in pay for those that stay, but no one loses a job.

[2]Yoshi Tsurumi, *The Dial,* September 1981.

Present Practice	Better Practice
Incentive pay. Pay based on performance.	**Abolish incentive pay and pay based on performance. Give everyone a chance to take pride in his work.**

Performance of the individual can not be measured, except possibly on a long-term basis. This we shall learn from the Red Beads (Ch. 7).

Reward for good performance may be the same as reward to the weather man for a pleasant day.

The effect of incentive pay is numbers and loss of focus on the aim.

Example: The top salesman may be a heavy loss to the company by overselling—selling to a customer a bigger copying machine than he (the customer) needs; selling a bigger or fancier insurance policy than the customer can handle; promising immediate delivery; promising unauthorized discount. Just as bad, the top salesman may sell a smaller copying machine than the customer needs, under the excuse that the customer argues that he can not afford to pay for the one that he needs. Either way, the customer holds a grudge against the company for selling to him the wrong machine.

Present Practice	Better Practice
Failure to manage the organization as a system. Instead, the components are individual profit centres. Everybody loses. Individuals, teams, divisions in the company work as individual profit centres, not for optimization of the aim of the whole organization. The various components thus actually rob themselves of long-term profit, joy in work, and other desirable measures of quality of life. The circumstance is in my experience accompanied by failure of communication. People have lost hope of ever understanding the relationship of their work to the work of others, yet they do not talk with each other.	Manage the company as a system (Chs. 3 and 4). Enlarge judiciously the boundaries of the system. The system must include the future. Encourage communication. Make physical arrangements for informal dialogue between people in the various components of the company, regardless of level of position. Encourage continual learning and advancement. Some companies have formed groups for comradeship in athletics, music, history, a language, etc., and have provided facilities for study-groups. The company can well afford to underwrite the cost of social gatherings in outside locations.

Education, industry, and government should interact as a system, with cooperation—win, win.

The first step in any organization is to draw a flow diagram to show how each component depends on others. Then everyone may understand what his job

is. If people do not see the process, they can not improve it. Anyone needs to see the process as a catwalk, a flow diagram—Paul Batalden, M.D., 13
November 1990.

Present Practice	Better Practice
M.B.O. (management by objective).	**Study the theory of a system. Manage the components for optimization of the aim of the system.**

In M.B.O., as practiced, the company's objective is
parceled out to the various components or divisions.
The usual assumption in practice is that if every component or division accomplishes its share, the whole company will accomplish the objective. This assumption is
not in general valid: the components are most always interdependent.

Unfortunately, efforts of the various components do
not add up. There is interdependence. Thus, the purchasing people may accomplish a saving of 10 per cent
over last year, and in doing so raise the costs of manufacture and impair quality. They may take advantage
of high-volume discount and thus build up inventory,
which will hamper flexibility and responsiveness to
meet unforeseen changes in the business.

Peter Drucker was clear on this point, with deep understanding. It is unfortunate that many people do not
bother to read his warning (*Management Tasks,
Responsibilities, Practices,* Harper & Row, 1973).

Horror story. A student told me that he took a course in the school of business at a prominent university in Washington. The students in the class learned how to use M.B.O., how to manage by results, how to rank people. He knew that all this was wrong, but he kept his mouth shut to avoid the possibility of F (for fail) for the course. Sadly, in the class were eight students from China, and other foreign students, learning what is wrong. They will go back home and tell everyone that they learned how Americans manage. How could they know that what they learned is wrong?

Present Practice	Better Practice
Setting numerical goals.	Work on a method for improvement of a process. By what method?

A numerical goal accomplishes nothing. Only the method is important, not the goal. By what method?

A numerical goal leads to distortion and faking, especially when the system is not capable to meet the goal. Anybody will meet the quota (goal) allotted to him. He is not responsible for the losses so generated.

Sears Roebuck waded into trouble in 1992 by allotting goals to their Auto Service Centers. Agents tried to meet the goals set for them. They did, to the detriment of the customer and of the reputation of the company. The fallacy lay in the goals set by management, not in the agents.

Instead of setting numerical quotas, management should work on improvement of the process. A flow diagram displays a process. The problem is how to improve it. The PDSA cycle will help (p. 132).

Quotas. Quotas for production are first cousins of numerical goals. The agent in San Francisco of one of our big banks had a quota: lend $83,000,000 per month. He did. The bank waded into trouble with bad loans. Can anyone blame an agent for doing his job? His livelihood depended on meeting his quota month by month.

A quota on the factory floor is hard to get rid of. Some people are able to complete their quotas in six hours. They then have two hours for TV, cards, reading. They like it that way. The game is numbers, not quality. This was good enough in the days when there was little competition, and quality was not a problem. Today, a quota is cause of worry to management, but it is hard to abolish. Examples appear on pages 72, 80, 81, in the book *Out of the Crisis*.

One way to move away from quotas is to introduce a horizontal production line, with a self-directed work force—anybody does anything that needs to be done. This plan smooths out the valleys caused by someone absent for any reason.

Present Practice	Better Practice
M.B.R. (management by results).	**Understand and improve the processes that produced the fault, defect, etc.**
Take immediate action on any fault, defect, complaint, delay, accident, breakdown.	**Understand the distinction between common causes of variation and special causes,**
Action on the last data-point.	**thus to understand the kind of action to take (*Out of the Crisis*, pp. 309ff.).**

The outcome of management by results is more trouble, not less.

What is wrong? Certainly we need good results, but management by results is not the way to get good results. It is action on outcome, as if the outcome came from a special cause. It is important to work on the causes of results—i.e., on the system. Costs are not causes: costs come from causes (Gipsie Ranney, 1988).

Example: Senior manager to a plant manager at eight o'clock every morning: What was your production yesterday? One thing sure, it was higher than it was the day before, or it was less. So what? What does the up or down mean?

In my experience, most troubles and most possibilities for improvement add up to proportions something like this:

94% belong to the system (the responsibility
of management)
6% are attributable to special causes

33

We shall understand these proportions after we do the experiment on the Red Beads (Ch. 7).

No amount of care or skill in workmanship can overcome fundamental faults of the system.

Present Practice	Better Practice
Buying materials and services at lowest bid (Point 4 of the 14 points).	Estimate the total cost of use of materials and services—first cost (purchase price) plus predicted cost of problems in use of them, their effect on the quality of final product.

There has been much publicity in the City of Washington about failure of equipment on the Metro. Someone pointed out that at least one moving stair in the duPont Circle Station is dependably out of order, dead. In contrast, one seldom sees a moving stair in London, Paris, Tokyo, or Moscow out of order.

The trouble in Washington was built in, guaranteed, by purchase of equipment at lowest bid. London, Paris, Tokyo, and Moscow were not hampered thus.

Procurement of goods and services for municipalities and other government agencies shows favor to local producers. The local producer thus runs on an inside track. The producer outside the area may in effect be shut out. Renewal of a contract, year after year, may appear to be a formality, as the relationship between supplier and customer grows tighter and tighter. This even tighter and tighter relationship will, under good management of producer and customer, ensure better and better quality and lower and lower costs as the years go by.

An example of low cost would be U.S. domestic postage, at this moment 29¢. It is the cheapest postage in the world. The service that it renders is the worst in any industrialized country in the world.

It might be better for some of us to pay higher postage, and to receive better service.

Present Practice	Better Practice
Delegate quality to someone, or to a group.	Accountability for quality rests with the top management.

Appointment of someone as Vice President in Charge of Quality will be disappointment and frustration. Accountability for quality belongs to top management. It can not be delegated.

Need for action. The magnitudes of the most important losses from action or inaction by management are unknowable (Lloyd S. Nelson; see *Out of the Crisis*, p. 20). We must nevertheless learn how to manage these losses. Failure to tackle them and to conquer them, and to transform management into line with the system of profound knowledge (Ch. 4) will only push us into further decline.

It is wrong to suppose that if you can't measure it, you can't manage it—a costly myth.

35

Do not confuse coincidence with cause and effect.[3] True: anyone could make a list of companies that are doing well, even though their management follows one or all of the above bad practices. These companies are saved by good luck, coincidence, having a product or service that commands good market. Any of these companies might do much better were the management to learn some theory of management.

If anyone were to study without theory such a company, i.e., without knowing what questions to ask, he would be tempted to copy the company, on the pretext that "they must be doing some things right." To copy is to invite disaster.

Likewise, one may find companies that are trying to do everything right, yet are having a hard time to survive. They would be still worse with bad management. How much worse, no one could know.

How far have we gone?   Careful thought concerning the origin and effects of the prevailing system of management will come forth with this question: Does anybody care about long-term profit?

Why do we ask a question like this? Every manager supposes that he is doing his best. He is, and this is the problem. His best is embedded in the present system of management, which as we have just learned, causes huge loss, of unknowable magnitude. His best efforts, without knowledge from outside, merely dig deeper the pit we are in.

---

[3]So stated by Gipsie Ranney at General Motors, 1993.

THEORY FOR LEADERSHIP OF THE TRANSFORMATION

Applications	Has penetrated?	Magnitude
Overall business strategy and planning	Not yet	
Companywide systems (personnel, training, systems of reward, merit pay, annual appraisal, pay for performance, legal, financial, purchase of materials, equipment, and services)	Not yet	Here are the big gains, 97%, waiting
Unique processes that produce figures	Yes	3%

The table above shows where we are and what remains to be done. The original draft of the table came from Dr. Edward M. Baker of the Ford Motor Company.

Somehow the theory for transformation has been applied mostly on the shop floor. Everyone knows about the statistical control of quality. This is important, but the shop floor is only a small part of the total. Anyone could be 100 per cent successful with the 3 per cent, and find himself out of business.

The most important application of the principles of statistical control of quality, by which I mean knowledge about common causes and special causes, is in the management of people (Ch. 6).

Ninety-five per cent of changes made by management today make no improvement. Examples are reorganization, a new computer. (Peter Scholtes, his 7th theorem, so he labeled it, January 1992.)

Beware of common sense. Common sense tells us to rank children in school (grade them), rank people on the job, rank teams, divisions, dealers, costs in hospitals. Reward the best, punish the worst. Punish with a day off without pay the ticket seller with the highest discrepancy for the month.

Common sense tells us to have quotas for people—or for groups—produce so many items per day, iron so many shirts in every hour or every day, the maids in a hotel allowed 20 minutes per room. An engineer must turn out a prescribed number of designs every month. Result: costs doubled, people robbed of pride of workmanship, no improvement possible.

Common sense tells us to speak to the operator about it when a customer reports something wrong with a product or with a service. "We have spoken to the operator about it; it won't happen again."[4]

Common sense tells us that if an item or service fails to

[4]William W. Scherkenbach, *The Deming Route* (George Washington University Continuing Engineering Education Press, Washington, 1986), p. 28.

meet requirements, take action, do something about it, and do it now. Do what?

Action taken today may only produce more mistakes tomorrow. It may be important to work on the process that produced the fault, not on him that delivered it.

Common sense tells us to reward the salesman of the month (the one that sold the most). Actually, he may be doing great harm to the company.

Salary for salesmen in place of commissions. Gallery Furniture Company of Houston put their salesmen on salary, in place of commission on sales. Result: steady increase in sales. Older salesmen now help beginners. Salesmen no longer try to steal business from other salesmen. They now help each other. They all help people in the warehouse to avoid scratches and breakage. They protect the customer, to make sure that he buys furniture suitable for his home and for the furniture already in it.

Result: sales go up month by month. Moreover, profit per square foot of floor space advances even faster.

Mr. Jim McInvale, manager, took my four-day seminar twice, from which he concluded that pay geared to sales was wrong, and that salaries for salesmen would be preferable.

A parallel example. The business of a company is distribution of several thousand products. Its customers are manufacturers. The company has 38 districts. The incentive was sales. The manager of each district was rewarded on sales. There was no cooperation. For example, one district would not transfer inventory to help another district to close a sale. District managers would invade each other's territory.

Management asked division managers every hour for figures on sales, with reasons for any decrease over the hour before.

Top management made a change: The managers of the districts went on salary. Result: sales up, up; cooperation, all inventories on file and switched by computer.

Figures come in, but the figures go on to charts to detect trends. The management now understand the distinction between common causes of variation, and special causes.

Under the former system, there was a bonus for extra amounts of sales. Some salesmen did well and got bonuses merely because the product that they sold was in high demand. Some salesmen did poorly because the product that they sold was in low demand.

On commission, focus was on sales. On salary, focus is on the customer. Customers now come in for business that in former days would not do business with this company.

The changes in this company began with the transformation of its president, Mr. Robert Rodin. His success up to transformation, so he believed, was his reliance on M.B.O., management by results, and incentive pay. He took my four-day seminar, and made the changes just described. He now tries to manage his company as a system.

Goals, aims, hopes. How could there be life without aims and hopes? Everyone has aims, hopes, plans. But a goal that lies beyond the means of its accomplishment will lead to discouragement, frustration, demoralization. In other words, there must be a method to achieve an aim. By what method?

When a company holds an individual accountable for a goal, it must provide to him the resources for accomplishment.

A company has aims, their statement of constancy of purpose.

Facts of life. There are facts of life that are not goals nor even aims. For example, if we do not reduce our mistakes and defective items to 3 per cent by the end of this year, we shall go out of business. This is not an aim. It is a fact of life. The whole company might, of course, put forth best efforts and build a method that they think will accomplish the reduction that is required to stay in business. In other words, the fact of life, a requirement for life, might be translated into a goal or an aim, provided a method for this accomplishment can be planned and carried out.

Futility of a numerical goal. A numerical goal accomplishes nothing, as already noted. What counts is the method—by what method? It is good to remember the admonition from Lloyd S. Nelson (*Out of the Crisis*, p. 20). If you can accomplish a goal without a method, then why were you not doing it last year? There is only one possible answer: you were goofing off.

A numerical goal is the apprehension of the highest desirable good, but for most mortals a practical impossibility (paraphrased from Caroline Alexander in the *New Yorker,* 16 December 1991, p. 83).

A picture may help. If the process is stable, then a numerical goal beyond the upper control limit is impossible. Figure 5 may help the reader to understand this statement. Output in the stable state varies day to day from common causes of variation. The upper control limit represents prediction of extreme output under the present process. To seek output beyond the upper control limit is as sensible as to defy gravity. The goal will be achieved only by improve-

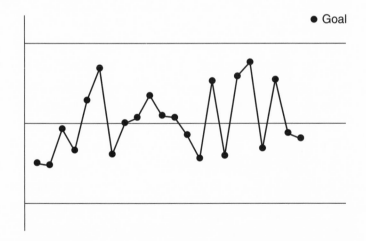

Fig. 5. The numerical goal lies beyond the upper control limit. It will not be achieved by the present process. (Taken from a paper delivered by Dr. Brian L. Joiner, 1987.)

ment of the present process, so that the new upper control limit will fall beyond the goal. What we need is methods for improvement of the process. The question is, BY WHAT METHOD? (Lloyd S. Nelson; see *Out of the Crisis*, p. 20.)

If there be no process, chaos in other words, anything can happen, for better or for worse. Prediction of performance of the process is impossible.

Will a numerical goal be achieved?   Anybody can achieve almost any goal by:
- Redefinition of terms
- Distortion and faking
- Running up costs

Pages 264–266 in the book *Out of the Crisis* show an example of fudged figures. The inspector was trying to save the jobs of three hundred people. Rumor had it amongst them that the plant manager had said that if the proportion defective that they produced ever went on any day to 10 per cent, he would close the place down and sweep it out. Whether he ever said that, or whether he would do it, are irrelevant speculations. All that matters is what the three hundred people and the inspector thought would happen. She never let the proportion defective go to 10 per cent. Her figures and the points on the chart that she plotted are imaginary. They are misleading, in illustration of the principle that wherever there is fear, there will be wrong figures. (More on p. 94.)

As another example, the manager of a grocery store is allowed only 1 per cent shrinkage (monetary value of goods that come into the store, minus the value of goods sold, measured on the same scale). He meets this allowance. How? Take people off the cash registers when a load of groceries comes in, send them to the back of the store to count cases and boxes and contents, compare with invoices, to avoid any undercount. Let paying customers wait in line at the front of the store. Never mind if they become restless and resolve never to come here again. Fat is cheap. Buy fat, and mix it with the meat. Who would know? Some customers do. Run short on fruits and vegetables that are slow movers and might spoil, unsold. Customers go elsewhere for these items. He knows 55 other ways to help to meet his allowance of 1 per cent shrinkage, all of which hurt the business. Can anybody blame him for living within his allowance? (Thanks to Professor John O. Whitney of Columbia University.)

A nuclear power plant sets a goal of no more than 11 accidents in a year. If there be danger to exceed this number, the management of the plant may defer maintenance, or engage an outside firm to do it. Let the accident show on his books, not on ours.

Goal: cut costs. A carrier of motor freight cuts costs by engaging cheap but unqualified clerks to compute freight charges. Result: a good customer discovers an inordinate number of mistakes. He engages an auditor to search for overcharges on the freight bills from this carrier. The carrier is required by government regulation in the United States and in Canada to refund any overcharge. The carrier thereupon engages an auditor to search his files for test of alleged overcharges, also for undercharges. The carrier does not send to the customer a bill for an undercharge less than $100. (There are exceptions. One carrier draws the line at $50, another at $15.) The carrier is thus obligated to pay any overcharge, and accepts the loss on most undercharges. He thus saves money on calculation of freight charges, and loses 20 times as much from mistakes. Result: heavy net loss.

Other examples appear in a paper by Joyce Orsini, "Bonuses: what is the impact?" *National Productivity Review*, Spring 1987.

Horrible example of numerical goals in public places. The bulletin *America 2000: An Educational Study,* published by the Secretary of Education, Washington, 18 April 1991, provides a horrible example of numerical goals, tests, rewards, but no method. By what method? Examples:

Numerical Goals

Page 9. The high school graduation rate will increase by the year 2000 to at least 90 per cent.

Every school in America will ensure that students learn …

Every adult American will be literate.

Every school will be free of drugs.

Page 15. The goal is to bring at least 535 … schools into existence by 1996.

Page 16. Whatever their approach, all new American schools will be expected to produce extraordinary gains in student learning. [By what method?]

Page 17. At least one new American school will be created in each congressional district by 1996.

Page 19. Performance standards for all federally aided adult education programs and holding programs accountable for meeting them.

More.

Report cards.[5] The government will exert further pressure by compiling results of these tests in public reports. This will allow comparisons of the performance of states and of the nation's 110,000 public schools. Again the idea is that citizens will demand progress.

Never mind the method. Manage by results. Wrong.

Page 32. Q. Do national tests mean a national curriculum?

A. No—although surveys and polls indicate that most Americans have no objection to the idea of a national curriculum. The American Achievement Tests will examine the results of education. They have nothing to say about how those results are produced, what teachers do in

[5] *Time*, 29 April 1991, p. 53.

class from one day to the next, what instructional materials are chosen, what lesson plans are followed. They should result in less regulation of the means of education, because they focus exclusively on the ends.

Merit Pay

Page 13. Merit schools program. Individual schools that make notable progress toward the national education goals deserve to be rewarded.

Page 14. Honor teachers ... reward outstanding teachers in all five ... core subjects.

Differential teacher pay: Differential pay will be encouraged for those who teach well, who teach core subjects, who teach in dangerous and challenging settings, or who serve as mentors for new teachers.

Page 12. Report cards on results. In addition to reports to parents on how their children are doing, report cards will also provide clear (and comparable) ... information on how schools, and school districts and states are doing.

What is wrong? Numerical goals accomplish nothing. Ranking and reward of individual people, schools, districts, do not improve the system. Only the method is important. By what method? Unfortunately, these goals have been posted in schools, giving pupils a bad start in life—goals without method.

The reader will try to be kind. The committee that wrote

this report put forth their best efforts, unaware that they needed knowledge. How could they know?

Note. *America 2000* was originally put together in December 1989 at the "Educational Summit" between the President and the governors of 50 states. These goals were published in February 1990 by the White House; later incorporated into *America 2000*.

This job may be an example of enlargement of a committee. We shall learn in Chapter 4 under Profound Knowledge that enlargement of a committee is not a way to acquire profound knowledge.

How could they know?

3

Introduction to a System[1]

> There is nothing better for a man to do than to eat and
> drink and enjoy himself in return for his labours.—
> Ecclesiastes 2, v. 24.

Aim of this chapter. We saw in the last chapter that we
are living under the tyranny of the prevailing style of management. Most people imagine that this style of management has always existed, and is a fixture. Actually, it is a
modern invention, a trap that has led us into decline. Transformation is required.

Education and government, along with industry, are also
in need of transformation.

The system of profound knowledge to be introduced in
the next chapter is a theory for transformation.

An integral part of the system of profound knowledge is
appreciation for a system, the aim of this chapter.

---

[1]This chapter and the next are in large part the work of Dr. Barbara
Lawton. It has also the benefit of critical contributions from Dr. Nida
Backaitis. The doctoral thesis of my student Cureton Harris, at New
York University, dated 1963, taught me much about American man-
agement. It is a pleasure to recommend to the reader the book *Intro-
duction to Operations Research,* by C. West Churchman, Russell L.
Ackoff, and E. Leonard Arnoff (John Wiley, 1957), in which pages 7
and 13 provide a clear start toward a system.

What is a system?   A system is a network of interdependent components that work together to try to accomplish the aim of the system.

A system must have an aim. Without an aim, there is no system. The aim of the system must be clear to everyone in the system. The aim must include plans for the future. The aim is a value judgment. (We are of course talking here about a man-made system.)

The components need not all be clearly defined and documented: people may merely do what needs to be done. Management of a system therefore requires knowledge of the interrelationships between all the components within the system and of the people that work in it.

A system must be managed. It will not manage itself. Left to themselves in the Western world, components become selfish, competitive, independent profit centres, and thus destroy the system.

The secret is cooperation between components toward the aim of the organization. We can not afford the destructive effect of competition.

Management's job.   It is management's job to direct the efforts of all components toward the aim of the system. The first step is clarification: everyone in the organization must understand the aim of the system, and how to direct his efforts toward it. Everyone must understand the danger and loss to the whole organization from a team that seeks to become a selfish, independent, profit centre.

Recommended aim. The aim proposed here for any organization is for everybody to gain—stockholders, employees, suppliers, customers, community, the environment—over the long term. For example, with respect to employees, the aim might be to provide for them good management, opportunities for training and education for further growth, plus other contributors to joy in work and quality of life.

Point 1 of the 14 points, the reader will recall, calls for a statement of constancy of purpose—the aim of the system, emphasis on purpose.

Is your organization a system? A company or other organization may have buildings, desks, equipment, people, water, telephones, electricity, gas, municipal services. But is it a system? In other words, is there an aim?

With some companies, because of short-term thinking, the only aim is survival for the day, with no thought about the future.

Development of aim.[2] Human beings have need for mobility, not for automobiles, trains, buses, or aeroplanes. Children have need for skills in reading, not for a certain curriculum, textbooks, or teaching technique. Choice of aim is clearly a matter of clarification of values, especially on the choice between possible options.

A system must create something of value, in other words, results. The intended results, along with consideration of

[2]Contributed by Carolyn Bailey.

recipients and of cost, mould the aim of the system. It is thus management's task to determine those aims, to manage the whole organization toward accomplishment of those aims.

It is important that an aim never be defined in terms of a specific activity or method. It must always relate to a better life for everyone.

The aim precedes the organizational system and those that work in it. Workers, for example, can not be the source of the aim, for how would one know what kind of workers to choose? Would one employ shoemakers or backhoe drivers to involve in determination of the aim? Choice of one or the other would imply that an aim already exists, even if not explicit.

It is an obligation of leadership to sponsor and energize the determination of the aim. The focus of this task could be in one person (such as an entrepreneur), or in a group (such as a board of directors), or investors. Wherever the point of origin, there must be, throughout the organization, a sense of agreement on the aim.

Management of a system. Anything less than direction of best efforts of everyone toward achievement of the aim or aims of the whole organization is a directed verdict toward failure to achieve best overall results. Everybody loses, even the people in a successful individual profit centre. (Examples to follow.) Management's job is thus clear— to achieve best results for everybody—everybody win. Time will bring changes that must be managed—must be predicted so far as possible. Growth in size and complexity of a system, and changes with time of external forces (competition, new product, new requirements) require overall management of efforts of components. An additional responsibility of management is to be ready to change the boundary of the system to better serve the aim. Changes may require redefinition of components.

Management of a system may require imagination. An example comes from the Department of Defense. The management of a group spent some of their meagre budget for better housing in a naval base, the theory being that without good housing, there would not be people there to fly the aeroplanes.

Another simple example in which one component operated at a loss for the good of the whole company, including the component that took the loss, comes from an observation that I made while doing some work years ago for the *Detroit News*. The food department of the *Detroit News* intentionally served food in the cafeteria so good and so cheap that employees ate their lunches in the company's cafeteria, attracted by quality and price. Employees thus spent far less time at lunch on the home ground, and more time on the job, than if they had gone out of the building for lunch. As I understood it, the food department lost an average of 60¢ per lunch, but the company as a whole came out ahead, not merely because employees spent more time on the job, but also for their appreciation of good management.

A system includes the future. Management and leaders have still another job, namely, to govern their own future, not to be merely victims of circumstance. We could refer here again to carburetors and vacuum tubes (pp. 9–10). As an example, instead of taking the loss from spurts in production to meet demand, followed by losses from valleys from decreased demand, it might be better to flatten production, or to increase production at an economical rate. Another possibility is to become agile and efficient in meeting peaks and valleys in demand. As another example, management may change the course of the company and of the industry by anticipation of needs of customers for new product or new service.

Preparation for the future includes lifelong learning for employees. It includes constant scanning of the environment (technical, social, economic) to perceive need for innovation, new product, new service, or innovation of method. A company can to some extent govern its own future.

What business ought we to be in five years from now? Ten years from now? Will we still be making carburetors (p. 10)?

Any system needs guidance from outside. Again, a system can not understand itself.

An organization may require someone in the position of aid to the president to teach and facilitate profound knowledge.

We have learned that a flow diagram is helpful toward understanding a system (pp. 19 and 21).

By understanding a system, one may be able to predict the consequences of a proposed change.

Boundary of a system. The boundary of the system to be described in Figure 6 (p. 58) may be drawn around a single company, or around an industry, or as in Japan in 1950, the whole country. The bigger be the coverage, the bigger be the possible benefits, but the more difficult to manage. The aim must include plans for the future.

An example of a whole industry as a system comes from William Ouchi's book *The M-Form Society* (Addison-Wesley, 1984), page 32. He was the keynote speaker at a meeting of a trade association in a beautiful resort north of Airport Miami. The meeting was held for three days— each day till noon, then out for fishing or golf. Dr. Ouchi explained to the group in his speech, on the morning of the first day, that he likes to go fishing now and then, and sometimes plays golf, but that it might be worthwhile to remark about the contrast between the activities of this group and that of their direct competitors in Japan.

Last month when I was in Tokyo, he explained, I attended meetings of your direct competitors, 200 companies, tiny and huge, working together as a system—working on design of products, export policy, tests of instruments, so that anybody's oscilloscope would agree with his customer's analyzer. They worked from eight in the morning till nine at night, 13 hours a day, five days a week: reached consensus after some months of labor.

Who do you think will be ahead five years from now, you or your Japanese competitors?

Would American companies dare to work together like this? Perhaps they could now, owing to the National Cooperative Research Act of 1984. However, American management must still learn that in order to compete, they must learn to cooperate (William W. Scherkenbach, *Deming's Road to Continual Improvement,* SPC Press, Knoxville, 1991). The Clayton Act had effectively prohibited this kind of cooperation.

A system includes competitors. Efforts by competitors, acting jointly or together, aimed at expanding the market and to meet needs not yet served, contribute to optimization for all of them. When the focus of competitors is to provide better service to the customer (e.g., lower costs, protection of the environment), everyone comes out ahead.

Typically, the management of a company spend a lot of time worrying about share of market. How big is our piece of the apple pie? How can we enlarge it at the expense of competition?

It would be better if all the competitors would use this time and energy to expand the market. They would all gain.

The three automotive companies in this country had together in 1960 a virtual monopoly. The management of the three companies spent time worrying about share of market. Where are we? How are we doing compared with our competitors? Better or worse than last month?

Better had all of them worked to expand the market, to make automobiles for a huge market not then served by the American companies. At that very time two million people in this country needed automobiles at lower first cost, dependable, and cheaper to run. Japanese auto makers came in and filled this market.

What ignited Japan? The flow diagram shown in Figure 6 was the spark that in 1950 and onward turned Japan around. It displayed to top management and to engineers a system of production. The Japanese had knowledge, great knowledge, but it was in bits and pieces, uncoordinated. This flow diagram directed their knowledge and efforts into a system of production, geared to the market—namely, prediction of needs of customers. The whole world knows about the results.

This simple flow diagram was on the blackboard at every conference with top management in 1950 and onward. It was on the blackboard in the teaching of engineers.

Action began to take place when top management and engineers saw how to use their knowledge.

Incidentally, Dr. S. Moriguti of Tokyo pointed out to me recently that 80 per cent of the capital of Japan was in attendance at every conference with top management, 1950 and after.

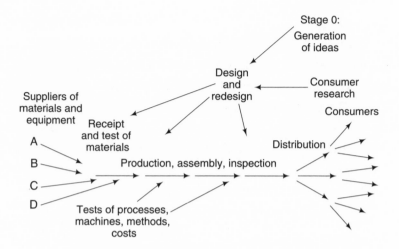

Fig. 6. Production viewed as a system. Improvement of quality envelops the entire production line, from incoming materials to the consumer, and redesign of product and service for the future. This chart was used in Japan in August 1950. In a service organization, the sources A, B, C, etc., could be sources of data, or work from preceding operations, such as charges (as in a department store), calculation of charges, deposits, withdrawals, inventories in and out, transcriptions, shipping orders, and the like.

The flow diagram starts with ideas about a possible product or service—what might the customer need; prediction. This is the 0-th stage, to be elaborated in Chapter 6.

This prediction leads to design of product or service. Will the market be sufficient to keep us in business?

Continuation through the cycle, including observations on use of the product in the hands of the customer, leads to redesign—new prediction. The cycle goes on and on, design and redesign. It is a cycle for continual learning and for continual adjustment.

Use of the flow diagram provides a feedback loop for continual improvement of product or service, and continual learning. We can observe the effect of redesign on costs, sales, and evaluation by the customer. (Contributed by Dr. Barbara Lawton and Dr. Nida Backaitis.)

Dynamics of a system. To make the flow diagram work, the flow of material and information from any part of the system must match the input requirements of the next stages. Thus, the aim in the flow diagram is for material to come in at the front, and to emerge at the end as usable product or service. The flow diagram in Figure 6 describes not only the flow of material, but also the flow of information needed to manage the system.

A flow diagram also assists us to predict what components of the system will be affected, and by how much, as a result of a proposed change in one or more components. (Contributed by Dr. Barbara Lawton.)

There are other flow diagrams in this book that the reader may wish to turn to: the Sacred Heart League on page 19, and development of an engine on page 134. The PDSA Cycle (p. 132) is a flow diagram for learning and for improvement of a process or of a product.

Joy in work. Suppose that we post names on Figure 6: you work here; John works there; I work here. Then everybody may see straightaway what his job is—whom do I depend on, who depends on me. Anyone may now understand how his work fits in with the work of other people. He may now engage his mind as well as his labor. He understands now what is meant by doing a good job. He may now take joy in his work.

This diagram, as an organization chart, is far more meaningful than the usual pyramid. The pyramid only shows responsibilities for reporting, who reports to whom. It shows the chain of command and accountability. A pyramid does not describe the system of production. It does not tell anybody how his work fits into the work of other people in the company. If a pyramid conveys any message at all, it is that anybody should first and foremost try to satisfy his boss (get a good rating). The customer is not in the pyramid. A pyramid, as an organization chart, thus destroys the system, if ever one was intended. (The observations in these two paragraphs come from Dr. Nida Backaitis.)

The pyramid contributes to fragmentation of the organization. In fragmentation, each component becomes an individual profit centre, destroying the system, more about which appears a few pages ahead.

My involvement in 1950 was at the invitation of JUSE (Union of Japanese Science and Engineering), then in embryonic stage. I had been in Japan in 1947 to work on the 1951 Census of Japan, and while there seized the opportunity to work also with the Japanese departments of agriculture, housing, and employment. These contacts facilitated acceptance of my message set forth in 1950, viz., the theory of a system, and cooperation.

Words from A. Richard Seebass.[3]

Agricultural research in the United States began with the Hatch Act in 1887, following England's success at Rothamsted. Experiment stations and agricultural extension agents in the United States began their work. They carry on research and make recommendations on what variety to plant, and when, how deep, spacing of rows, fertilization, effect of rainfall, irrigation when and how.

They carry out research on fruit, and on production of milk, meat, wool. Recommendations and technology are transferred by county agricultural agents to farmers. Farmers have always been quick to learn and to change. They have adopted without hesitation any labor-saving device or machinery. They have always practiced cooperation.

Knowledge about agricultural practices has spread to developing countries. Yield has improved year by year in some of these countries, diminishing the demand for food from North America. [Knowledge crosses borders without a visa.]

No such parallel exists between agriculture and industry. No such spread of knowledge from

[3]Dean of Engineering, University of Colorado.

America to Japan took place when Dr. Deming went there in 1950 at their request to help Japanese industry with quality. What he taught in Japan did not exist in America. He did not export to Japan American methods. He taught there the principle of a system. Japanese management and engineers listened and learned, put into practice what he taught. He relied on cooperation between people and between companies. Cooperation has always been in Japan a way of life.

The boundary of the system would be all Japan, Deming taught them. Companies must work together in cooperation. As you learn, teach others. The transformation in Japan must be a prairie fire covering the whole country.

(End of statement by Dean Seebass.)

A system of schools. A system of schools (public schools, private schools, parochial schools, trade schools, universities, for example) is not merely pupils, teachers, school boards, boards of regents, and parents working separately to achieve their own aims. It should be, instead, a system in which these groups work together to achieve the aims that the community has for the school—growth and development of children, and preparation for them to contribute to the prosperity of society.

It should be a system of education in which pupils from toddlers on up through the university take joy in learning, free from fear of grades and gold stars, and in which teachers take joy in their work, free from fear in ranking. It should be a system that recognizes differences between pupils and differences between teachers. Such a system of schools would be destroyed if some group of schools decided to band together to lobby for their own special interests. They together with all other schools would in time be losers.

Delayed effects. The effect of a movement by management made now may not take effect till many months have passed, even years. The immediate effect may be nigh zero, or even negative. Interpretation of the change could thus be elusive.

A simple example is training. The only immediate evidence is its cost, expense. The effect of training will not be realized for months or even years in the future. Moreover, the effect can not be measured.

Then why does a company spend money for training? Because the management believe that there will in the future be benefits that far outweigh the cost. In other words, the management are guided by theory, not by figures. They are wise.

An unstudied solution to a problem may yield immediate results in the right direction, yet in time bring disaster. For example, to sack people lowers costs straightaway, but in due time may cause serious consequences. The benefits of a fundamental solution may not show up for a long time.

A diagram on page 106 of Peter Senge's book *The Fifth Discipline* (Doubleday, 1990) illustrates this point.

Interdependence and interaction. An important job of management is to recognize and manage the interdependence between components. Resolution of conflicts, and removal of barriers to cooperation, are responsibilities of management.

Job description needs revision. A job description must do more than prescribe motions, do this, do that, this way, that way. It must tell what the work will be used for, how this work contributes to the aim of the system.

Suppose that you tell me that my job is to wash this table. You show to me soap, water, and a brush. I still have no idea what the job is. I must know what the table will be used for after I wash it. Why wash it? Will the table be used to set food on? If so, it is clean enough now. If it is to be used for an operating table, I must wash the table several times with scalding water, top, bottom, and legs; also the floor below it and around it.

Another example: I could do a much better job (fewer mistakes) if I knew what the program is to be used for. The specifications don't tell me what I need to know (computer programmer).

Anyone on a job needs to understand in detail the work and needs of the people that come after him in the flow diagram (catwalk) of the work of the organization.

An example of failure of this principle is the buttons on the arm of the seat in an aeroplane. The man that put the buttons in place obviously never rode in an aeroplane. How may the passenger turn his light on or off? The passenger may by good luck and dogged perseverance, trying this button and that, discover the secret. Why should it be a puzzle to turn a light on or off?

The man that designed the pocket calendar that I am using never used a pocket calendar. If he had, he would not fill up spaces with useless information, but would leave them blank, for notes that the user may wish to make.

St. Paul understood a system. Excerpts from 1 Corinthians 12:8.

> A body is not one single organ, but many. Suppose that the foot should say, "Because I am not a hand, I do not belong to the body," it does belong to the body none the less. Suppose that the ear were to say, "Because I am not an eye, I do not belong to the body," it does still belong to the body. If the body were all eye, how could it hear? If the body were all ear, how could it smell?... there are many different organs, but one body. The eye can not say to the hand, "I do not need you."[4]

Destruction of a system. (Contributed by Dr. Nida Backaitis.) Now, suppose that we take the flow diagram (organization chart) of Figure 6 and break it up into competitive components—consumer research for one, design

[4]Called to my attention by Dr. Nida Backaitis at Westminster Abbey, 11 July 1990, this passage being in the second lesson appointed for Evensong for the 11th day of the month, as it has been for centuries.

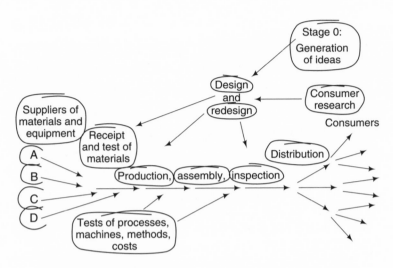

Fig. 7. This is Figure 6 broken into competitive components. The system is destroyed. (Contributed by Dr. Nida Backaitis.)

of product another, redesign another, each supplier for himself, etc. (Fig. 7). Every component now becomes competitive with the others. Each one now does his best, by some competitive measure, to make a mark for himself. Can anyone blame him? This is his only hope of survival.

Result: The system is destroyed, causing loss of unknowable magnitude.

A common example of demolition of a system is pressure of a congressman for a federal project to go to his state, regardless of what would be best for the country as a whole.

Another example is pressure that he exerts to hold on to a naval base in his state, when Congress has decreed national reduction in naval bases. Can you blame him? Reelection depends on his success to hold on to a naval base in his state, regardless of what is best for the nation as a whole.

A possible solution would be to elect a congressman for life, or to age 90. Another solution might be to limit his term of office to 10, 12, or 15 years, reelection barred. Such a suggestion could be construed as an example of tampering (Ch. 9)—action on the system without action on the fundamental cause of the trouble. The fundamental cause of the trouble is failure of people to understand that what is best for the whole country is identical with what in the long run is best for everybody.

An example of destruction of a system.   Engine and transmission both had electrical components in them. An engineer with great knowledge redesigned some of the components, and found that by putting other and different electrical components in the engine, none would be needed in the transmission. The following table portrays the alternatives.

ELECTRICAL COMPONENTS

Status	Engine	Transmission	Both
As is	$100	$80	$180
Proposed	$130	$ 0	$130
Gain from proposal			$ 50

The proposal was rejected by the financial people associated with the engine, because the proposal would increase by $30 the cost of the engine. Their job was to decrease costs of the engine, not to increase them. That the proposal would decrease overall costs of the whole company by $50 was not a factor to consider by the financial people associated with the engine. Their job was with the engine, not the vehicle. The engine was to them an individual profit centre.

Another example of destruction of a system. A woman called me in Washington by telephone from Chicago. She knew that I should be in New York the next Monday to teach at Columbia University and at New York University. She wished to have a half hour of my time. She would arrive in New York at 7 Monday morning, and could meet me anywhere in New York at whatever time I might specify. The purpose of her trip to New York was to attend a meeting there on behalf of her company Monday afternoon and Tuesday, to deliver a paper and to exchange thoughts with colleagues. Some arithmetic flitted into my head.

> 0700 h New York time, arrive at LaGuardia
>   Field
> 0430 h New York time, be on board in
>   Chicago
> 0330 h Chicago time, be on board in Chicago
> 0130 h Chicago time, leave home
> 0030 h Chicago time, out of bed

Why bother to go to bed? She would arrive at New York wholly unfit for the meeting in the afternoon. Why not arrive at 11:30 or noon, and get some sleep? Any other flight, she explained, would cost her $138. Her travel department gets a low rate on the flight specified.

Would it not be better for the company as a whole (and hence for everybody in the company) for the travel department to understand that their job is to put the traveller down at destination physically fit for the job? Here is the score:

As managed now:

Travel department   +   Traveller – – – –

Better management:

Travel department   –   Traveller + + + +

With better management, there would be higher earnings to support increases in pay for everybody, including the travel department.

Think what this great company could be with improvement in management!

Another example. The trip by air from LaGuardia Field in New York to Orlando requires two hours, nonstop. (I made it myself only last week.) I learned that a woman, on company business, made the trip next day in seven hours. Her travel department had negotiated a low rate that required change of aeroplanes in two cities enroute. She lost five hours. The score:

> Travel department   +   Traveller − − − −
> The company − − −

The travel department, by doing their job, created a loss to the company. As a result, everybody is a loser, including the people in the travel department.

Can you blame the travel department for saving money when that is their job? No. Where is the problem? Management that does not understand a system.

An automotive company divided itself into two divisions, traditionally:

1. Small cars, lower level in price
2. Luxury, heavier cars, higher price

There was of course some overlap.

Then came a policy of top management to play one division against the other, under the supposition that competition between the two divisions would lead to better automobiles and brisk sales. The pay of the top people in the two divisions would depend on sales. To increase sales, the division that was noted for small economical cars extended their line to include a battleship. For the same reason, the division that was noted for heavier luxury cars extended their line into light cars. The extensions unfortunately eroded the company's reputation for quality. The top management eventually, gradually, and grudgingly acknowledged that competition between the two divisions was the wrong fork in the road, and terminated dependence of pay on sales.

Yet another example of destruction of a system. Cureton Harris, in pursuit of her doctorate at New York University (thesis dated 1963) described a system for a company, how the various components should work together for optimization of profit and joy in work. She visited the people in various departments and divisions in 11 companies between New York and Philadelphia with the aim to learn how the various departments or divisions work together.

She discovered (e.g.) that the people engaged in design and redesign of product or service did not talk to the people engaged in consumer research. To talk with them might suggest to the management that we don't know our business here: we had to ask for help from those people in consumer research. Let there never be any suspicion that we don't possess knowledge necessary for our work. She found independent competitive centres everywhere. The various departments and divisions destroyed the system that might have existed. There was one exception, the Scott Paper Company in Philadelphia.

Everything best is not enough. Dr. Russell Ackoff pointed out years ago that if anyone were to assemble the best parts for an automobile, disregarding for every part its price tag and source, the parts would not make an automobile. They would not form a system.

Mr. H. R. Carabelli of Michigan Bell Telephone Company remarked to me that a company could have the best product engineer, the best manufacturing engineer, the best man in the country in marketing, yet if these men do not work together as a system, the company could be swallowed whole by the competition with people far less qualified, but with good management.

If the various components of an organization are all optimized (each for individual profit, each a prima donna), the organization will not be.

If the whole is optimized, the components will not be.

Destruction of schools. A public school in the United States is not operated as a component of a system. Optimization is obstructed by a city superintendent, a county superintendent, a school board (elected, shifting over time, no constancy of purpose), district board, local government, county government, state board of education, federal government, assessment by standardized tests of pupils, comparisons between districts and states.

Who would wish to do business with a loser? A woman wrote to me as follows:

> My marriage went from rough to rocky, rougher to rockier, eternal trouble, win, lose, each one jockeying to be the winner. I took your seminar and learned about a system, cooperation, win, win. I explained it to my husband. We thereupon worked together on every detail, seeking win, win: both of us win. We both won. Who would wish to compete in a marriage? The winner would be married to a loser. Who would wish to be married to a loser?

This letter raises a good question: who would wish to do business with a loser? Would anyone wish for his supplier to be a loser? his customer? his employees? the employees of his supplier, of his customers? Of course not.

Family life. The transformation affects family life. Parents will not rank their children, nor show special favors or rewards. Would parents wish for one child to be a loser? Would his brothers and sisters be happy to have a loser in the family? Transformed, the family will be a living demonstration of cooperation in the form of mutual support, love, and respect.

Failure of adversarial competition. If economists understood the theory of a system, and the role of cooperation in optimization, they would no longer teach and preach salvation through adversarial competition. They would, instead, lead us into the best plan for a system, in which everybody would come out ahead.

Anyone would agree with me, I think, that our air service in the United States is deplorable, an example of what is predictable from deregulation, competition, and open entry. Could it be worse? Wait a month.

Price fixing. If a monopoly or any two or more companies or institutions that dominate a market were to put their heads together for uniform prices, they would be fools to set the price a cent higher than what would be best in the long run for the whole system—they themselves, their customers, suppliers, employees, environment, and the com-

73

munities that their people work in. They would only cheat themselves out of profit in the long run were they to set the price any higher.

Equally, if a monopoly or group of people that dominate a market were to hold off the market any new device or service, aiming at maximum profit in the short run, they would only cheat themselves out of long-term profit, and would cheat their customers, their suppliers, and the employees out of their rightful gain.

The function of the Antitrust Division should be to explain this principle. In other words, their function should be education, to achieve maximum benefit from monopolies and cartels. This would be far better than to spend time in search of imaginary violators as victims.

There should be provision for open forum on prices. Producers and customers would work together. They would exchange figures and points of view. Any customer should have the privilege to review and to protest a suggested price.

Any price decided upon today may, because of new knowledge, new figures, or because of technological developments, require reconsideration tomorrow.

Suppose the aim of a company were short-term profit. Set the price as high as the traffic will bear. Make a big profit in a hurry and get out. A useful function of the Antitrust Division would then be protection of society.

Some remarks on monopolies. A monopoly has the best chance to be of maximum service to the world, and has a heavy obligation to do so. Maximum service requires, of course, enlightened management. The contributions to our welfare of monopolies have been great. One need only think of the contributions of the Bell Telephone Laboratories, a monopoly, responsible only to themselves. What would the world be without the contributions of the Bell Telephone Laboratories?

Everybody in the United States is an innocent victim of the destruction by the Antitrust Division of the telephone system that the United States enjoyed till 1984. A monopoly it was. It was also the envy of the world.

We no longer have a telephone system. We have telephones.

Open entry is not the road to salvation. To compete with the long lines of AT&T, a company would face barriers. A competitor would require tremendous investment in circuits, research, advertising. If he were successful in capturing a sizable share of the long distance market, he and AT&T would both operate at higher cost than one of them alone as a monopoly. Long distance rates would go up. We would all pay. We would all lose. There would be no winner.[5]

Cooperation of Ivy League universities. The Antitrust Division accused in 1992 a number of universities in the

[5]Kosaku Yoshida, "New Economic Principles in America—Competition and Cooperation," *Columbia Journal of Business,* Winter 1992, *vol. xxvi, no. iv.*

United States of working together to arrive at uniform figures for financial aid to students, as if cooperation like this is a sin against the American people. Actually, this kind of cooperation should be encouraged, as it is a service in the interest of students.

Another wrong of the Antitrust Division against the people of the United States was to break up years ago AT&T and the Western Union Telegraph Company.

An example of a monopoly, well managed, is the de Beers Consortium, which for over a century has dominated the market for diamonds. They own the Kimberley mine. They have persistently held the price of diamonds low, and have found uses for diamonds. They and the rest of the world have been beneficiaries of this good judgment.

If de Beers and General Electric wish to work together on the prices of diamonds, they should be encouraged to do so, provided they understand a system in which everybody wins.

An example of cooperation that may bear fruit is the European Community. There are problems at the start, because some industries must take short-term losses in order to build the European Community. There should be some way to protect stockholders in these industries, and to protect employees thrown out of work.

The U.S. Postal Service is not a monopoly. The authorities of the postal service are hampered by Congress. If the U.S. Postal Service were a monopoly, there would be a chance of better service.

Remarks on a system of transportation. The U.S. Interstate Commerce Commission (I.C.C.) took to court in September 1990 the heads of the 10 rate bureaus for motor freight, accusing them of price fixing. The rate bureaus, through their General Counsel Bryce Rea, Esq., of Washington, asked me to write a statement to try to explain how the Interstate Commerce Commission has the obligation to support a system of intercity motor freight, and to guide it. My statement follows.

INVESTIGATION OF MOTOR CARRIER COLLECTIVE RATE
MAKING AND RELATED PROCEDURES AND PRACTICES

Statement of Dr. W. Edwards Deming
before the Interstate Commerce Commission

Ex Parte MC-196
23 August 1990

I

No documentation is required to show that the United States' position in world markets has declined. The growing economic challenge from outside our shores is very real and is not about to disappear.

As I see it, the issue is quality—quality of product, quality of service, quality of work environment, and quality of cooperation between government and industry. This nation is at a crossroads in terms of our resolve to recognize and meet the challenge. Transformation is required. Transformation will not be spontaneous.

I have been associated with the motor freight industry for over 35 years, and I view its declining economic health with increasing concern. Could it be that this decline may in large part be attributed to the Commission's emphasis on competition for price, above all else?

II

The rate bureaus provide a forum for discussion among concerned shippers and carriers. Any collectively made rates are subject to shipper protest and review by the Commission. As to such rates, I am confident that motor carriers are mindful of my admonitions that were they to set collective prices any higher than what would optimize the whole system—carriers, shippers, communities—they would only cheat themselves out of profit, and deprive the communities that they serve, their employees, and the environment, of the benefits of earnest commitment to quality and cost-efficient service. Prices higher than what would optimize the whole system would turn customers toward other means of transport.

III

Efficient transportation must not be judged by price alone. Cheaper is not always better. Far more important to the user of transportation service is reliability and dependability. This includes narrower and narrower variation in time of delivery. It also means narrower and narrower variation in time of transit. It means lower costs in the long run (Fig. 8).

Wide variations in time of delivery require the customer to lay in heavy inventories in order to keep production steady in spite of late delivery. Early deliveries are costly. The customer must find warehousing space until the goods are needed. Narrower and narrower distribution time should be an aim.

To accomplish such aims, the carrier must maintain equipment in good order. He may not run power units and his employees to exhaustion. Real improvement in quality of service necessitates that the carriers be able to run consistently from point to point without breakdown of equipment or impairment of efficiency of employees.

IV

The time has come to understand and manage transportation as a system. The system here consists of several components—the carriers, the shippers that they serve, employees of both, communities that they live in, the environment, the nation as a whole, and government agencies involved—the I.C.C. These components are interdependent.

A system requires an aim. Without an aim, there is no system. The aim is value judgment. In our increasingly competitive world, I suggest the following as the aim of our transportation system:

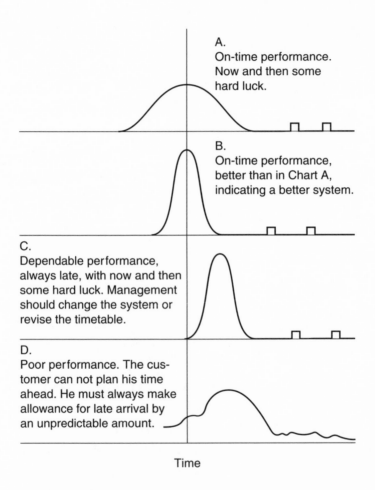

A.
On-time performance.
Now and then some
hard luck.

B.
On-time performance,
better than in Chart A,
indicating a better system.

C.
Dependable performance,
always late, with now and then
some hard luck. Management
should change the system or
revise the timetable.

D.
Poor performance. The customer can not plan his time
ahead. He must always make
allowance for late arrival by
an unpredictable amount.

Time

Fig. 8. Some possible distributions of time of delivery.
(Taken from *Out of the Crisis,* p. 477.)

1. Better and better service—that is, more dependable delivery. Continual improvement in on-time delivery.
2. Lower and lower cost to the carrier.
3. Better quality of life for employees of carriers and shippers.
4. Protection of the environment.

By focusing on a system of quality, everybody wins. This aim is not wild fantasy. It can be accomplished. Carriers, shippers, their employees, must work together for optimization of the system. Left to themselves, individual components will not accomplish the aim. They will, instead, defeat it, and everybody will lose over the long run.

A system must be managed. It must be led.

Competition should be directed toward expansion of the market and to meet needs not yet served. Given a system focus, carriers will fit themselves into the quest for quality and optimization.

Cooperation between shippers and carriers and between carriers as components in transportation is necessary.

V

The I.C.C. is in unique position to recognize the increasing challenge of world competition, and the need for transformation in transportation to assist U.S. producers to meet that challenge. That transformation will not be spontaneous. It will not be accomplished simply by playing one carrier off against another to achieve lower prices.

The Commission must recognize that competition based on the premise of a zero-sum game will destroy, not foster, a healthy transportation system. Profits must exist, and industry must work as a team in which all participants, large and small, survive and prosper. American business is faced with an increasingly vigorous competitive challenge from industry throughout the world. Only through steadfast commitment to cooperation, for optimization of the whole, and through resolution by all facets of American business, large and small, to improve, can this challenge be met. Shippers and carriers require direction and guidance.

The key is thorough commitment to quality throughout the transportation system. I urge the I.C.C. to undertake the role of leadership to promote cooperation between the various components of transportation, and responsiveness to the need of cooperation. The aim would be continual improvement of service to shippers, continual improvement of quality of service, and stability in the industry of motor freight. It seems to me that the responsibility for the leadership required rests with the I.C.C. Who else could do it?

(End of statement to the I.C.C.)

Illustration of selfish competition versus cooperation between departments. Harm comes from internal competition and conflict, and from the fear that is thereby generated. A manager of purchasing, under pressure to reduce costs, changes to a cheaper source. Engineering Design imposes unnecessarily tight tolerances to compensate for the fact that Manufacturing never reaches the standards asked of it. Departments performing better than budget start spending near the end of the year because they know that otherwise their next year's budget will be reduced. As the end of the month looms, salesmen start doing every-thing they can to meet their quotas, with scant regard to the problems caused to Manufacturing, Administration, and Delivery, let alone to the customer. Figures are massaged, computations redefined, so that reports show more of what senior management wish to see.

Tables 1 to 4 illustrate loss in the environment of conflict, and gain from cooperation.[6]

The reader may wish at this point to turn to the exercise on the principles of management of components as individ-ual profit centres, and for maximum contribution to the company as a whole (and hence to themselves as well), pre-sented by William W. Scherkenbach in his book *Deming's Road to Continual Improvement* (SPC Press, Knoxville, 1991), pp. 171–173.

Another reference to recommend is the book by J. William Pfeiffer and John E. Jones, *Win As Much As You Can* (University Associates, San Diego, 1980), with my thanks to Dr. Wendy Coles.

---

[6] The opening paragraph here and the tables and text are taken from the book by Henry R. Neave, *The Deming Dimension* (SPC Press, Knoxville, 1990), pp. 232–239. The origin of these tables came in 1988 from Mr. Fred Z. Herr, then Vice President of Product Assurance in the Ford Motor Company. Dr. Neave acknowledges help from Dr. Nida Backaitis.

Table 1.   For the purpose of this example, our company has three departments: purchasing, manufacturing, sales. We call them A, B, C. The left-hand column lists plans that each area has made to improve its performance. Under the prevailing style of management, each area naturally adopts a plan that is beneficial to itself, without consideration of any other area. Other possible plans have no chance of adoption. No one knows nor cares about any other area, hence in Table 1 there are no entries under other areas.

Table 1

Areas and their plans	Effect on Area A	Effect on Area B	Effect on Area C	Net effect on the company
Area A i ii iii	+ + +			
Area B i ii		+ +		
Area C i ii iii			+ + +	

In Table 2, we know and show the effects on other areas from the plans made in Table 1, and the effects on the company as a whole. Plans that are beneficial to any one area may well be detrimental for other areas. The net effect on the company turns out to be two negatives, negative two million dollars we may call it. Distributed equally, each area loses $670,000.

Table 2

Areas and their plans	Effect on Area A	Effect on Area B	Effect on Area C	Net effect on the company
Area A				
i	+	−	−	−
ii	+	−	+	+
iii	+	−	−	−
Area B				
i	−	+	−	−
ii	+	+	−	+
Area C				
i	+	−	+	+
ii	−	−	+	−
iii	−	−	+	−
Net effect of plans adopted	+ +	− − − −	0	− −
Distribution of benefits	−0.67	−0.67	−0.67	−2

In Table 3, each area, now under enlightened top management, seeks maximum benefit to the whole company, plusses in the column at the right. Only plans with predicted positive impact on the company as a whole are acted on. Everybody now wins, including areas that take a loss for the benefit of the whole company. In the distribution of benefits (bottom row), every area receives $1,000,000.

Table 3

Plan selected	Areas and their plans	Effect on Area A	Effect on Area B	Effect on Area C	Net effect on the company
ii	Area A i ii iii	 + + +	 − − −	 − + −	 − + −
ii	Area B i ii	 − +	 + +	 − −	 − +
i	Area C i ii iii	 + − −	 − − −	 + + +	 + − −
	Net effect of plans adopted	+ + +	−	+	+ + +
	Distribution of benefits	1	1	1	3

Success in Table 3 leads to exploration of plans that previously never saw the light of day (Table 4). Amongst this greater range of plans, some produce net benefit to the whole company. Some plans, intended to be beneficial to the whole company, turn out upon examination to be failures. The net results of the plans selected show in the bottom line of Table 4 heavy gain for the company as a whole. Every area gains $2,670,000.

Table 4

Plan selected	Areas and their plans	Effect on Area A	Effect on Area B	Effect on Area C	Net effect on the company
	Area A				
	i	+	−	−	−
ii	ii	+	−	+	+
	iii	+	−	−	−
iv	iv	−	+	+	+
v	v	−	+	+	+
	vi	−	−	+	−
	Area B				
	i	−	+	−	−
ii	ii	+	+	−	+
iii	iii	+	−	+	+
iv	iv	+	−	+	+
	Area C				
i	i	+	−	+	+
	ii	−	−	+	−
	iii	−	−	+	−
iv	iv	+	+	−	+
	v	+	−	−	−
	Net effect of plans adopted	+ + + +	0	+ + + +	+ + + + + + + +
	Distribution of benefits	2.67	2.67	2.67	8

Some common examples of cooperation. Competition leads to loss. People pulling in opposite directions on a rope only exhaust themselves: they go nowhere. What we need is cooperation. Every example of cooperation is one of benefit and gains to them that cooperate. Cooperation is especially productive in a system well managed. It is easy to make a list of examples of cooperation, some of which are so natural that we may not have recognized them as cooperation. Everybody wins.

1. The time of day, based on Greenwich mean time. You and your competitor and your customers use the same time signals.

2. The date, 29 November, based on the international date line. You and your competitor and your customers use the same date.

3. Red and green traffic lights, the same meaning the world over, the red light above the green.

4. The metric system, used the world over.

5. The ratio of the focal length of a lens to its diameter refers the world over to wavelength 546 nanometres. (For an anachromatic lens, the ratio is valid for any wavelength in the visible spectrum.)

6. The American Society for Testing and Materials (A.S.T.M.) and other standardizing bodies. Here in my hand is a magnifying glass, with a light. Press a button, illumination. If the batteries need replacement, I may buy AAA batteries anywhere in this world. They will fit. I

may get stung on quality, but they will fit. What if I had to order tailor-made batteries? I would not own the instrument.

7. Licensing of a process or product to some other company.

8. Companies make parts and products for each other. Almost any chemical company is dependent on competitors for intermediate products. Automotive companies make parts or even whole engines or transmissions for each other. I have in mind a division in one of our automotive companies in which a competitor is this division's best customer.

9. A large data-processing company does work for small companies that are not equipped for some jobs. Both companies win, and the customer too.

10. Meetings of scientists and other professional people, at which speakers and participants contribute to other members' new theory and methods, with exchange of theory and experience.

11. Journals, articles in which authors share with the world new ideas, new methods, new results.

12. A railway car may move from Halifax to Montreal to Boston, to Toronto, back down through Buffalo, Kansas City, Miami, Houston, into Mexico, to San Diego, Los Angeles, San Francisco, Portland, Seattle, Vancouver, Calgary, Saskatoon, Edmonton, Winnipeg, Duluth, Chicago, Kansas City—same gauge, matching systems of brakes and

of drawbars. Result: lower costs of transportation, more dependable performance.

13. Cooperation between professional men, any of them ready to help another.

14. We buy a light bulb, or an electric heater, curling iron, refrigerator, 110 volts, 60 cycles. This is standard voltage over all North America, and the plug will fit our outlet. Result: advantages of mass production; also convenience.

15. **A personal example.** My automobile, sitting in front of my house, would not start. I called Bill at the Exxon station not far away. When the man from the Exxon station came, I noted that he was in a truck owned by his competitor across the street. How smart these people are, I perceived. Each station owns one truck. By borrowing the competitor's one and only truck, if it be idle, both stations provide to their customers service equivalent to ownership of perhaps 1.8 trucks, at the cost of owning only one. Advantages: these stations both retain business of customers at lowest cost. Even further cooperation: one station stays open late one night, the other stays open late the next night. Result: they both retain business; a late customer need not drive to some other part of town to fill his tank.

The reader may note that the result of every example of cooperation is that everybody wins.

Dr. Shewhart often said that differences in building codes city to city in Europe were far more effective than tariffs in raising costs and depriving the people of Europe of the advantages of mass production. These differences will be eliminated through establishment of the European Community.

4

A System of Profound Knowledge[1]

And the chaff he will burn with unquentiable fire.—
Luke 3, 17.

Aim of this chapter. The prevailing style of management must undergo transformation. A system can not understand itself. The transformation requires a view from outside. The aim of this chapter is to provide an outside view— a lens—that I call a system of profound knowledge. It provides a map of theory by which to understand the organizations that we work in.

The first step. The first step is transformation of the individual. This transformation is discontinuous. It comes from understanding of the system of profound knowledge. The individual, transformed, will perceive new meaning to his life, to events, to numbers, to interactions between people.

Once the individual understands the system of profound knowledge, he will apply its principles in every kind of relationship with other people. He will have a basis for judg-

---

[1] The text of this chapter is in large part the work of Dr. Barbara Lawton. The diagram on p. 97, with the bowling team and the orchestra, is hers. I am deeply indebted also to Dr. Nida Backaitis for much help.

ment of his own decisions and for transformation of the organizations that he belongs to. The individual, once transformed, will:

Set an example
Be a good listener, but will not compromise
Continually teach other people
Help people to pull away from their current practice and beliefs and move into the new philosophy without a feeling of guilt about the past

The outside view. The layout of profound knowledge appears here in four parts, all related to each other:

- Appreciation for a system
- Knowledge about variation
- Theory of knowledge
- Psychology

One need not be eminent in any part nor in all four parts in order to understand it and to apply it. The 14 points for management (*Out of the Crisis,* Ch. 2) in industry, education, and government follow naturally as application of this outside knowledge, for transformation from the present style of Western management to one of optimization.

Preliminary remarks. The various segments of the system of profound knowledge proposed here can not be separated. They interact with each other. Thus, knowledge of psychology is incomplete without knowledge of variation.

A manager of people needs to understand that all people are different. This is not ranking people. He needs to understand that the performance of anyone is governed largely by the system that he works in, the responsibility of management. A psychologist that possesses even a crude understanding of variation as will be learned in the experiment with the Red Beads (Ch. 7) could no longer participate in refinement of a plan for ranking people.

Further illustrations of entwinement of psychology and use of the theory of variation (statistical theory) are boundless. For example, the number of defective items that an inspector finds depends on the size of the work load presented to him (documented by Harold F. Dodge in the Bell Telephone Laboratories around 1926). An inspector, careful not to penalize anybody unjustly, may pass an item that is just outside the borderline (*Out of the Crisis*, p. 266). The inspector in the illustration on page 265 of the same book, to save the jobs of 300 people, held the proportion of defective items below 10 per cent. She was in fear for their jobs.

A teacher, not wishing to penalize anyone unjustly, will pass a pupil that is barely below the requirement for a passing grade.

Fear invites wrong figures. Bearers of bad news fare badly. To keep his job, anyone may present to his boss only good news.

A committee appointed by the President of a company will report what the President wishes to hear. Would they dare report otherwise?

An individual may inadvertently seek to cast a halo about himself. He may report to an interviewer in a study of readership that he reads the *New York Times,* when actually this morning he bought and read a tabloid.

Statistical calculations and predictions based on warped figures may lead to confusion, frustration, and wrong decisions.

Accounting-based measures of performance drive employees to achieve targets of sales, revenue, and costs, by manipulation of processes, and by flattery or delusive promises to cajole a customer into purchase of what he does not need (adapted from the book by H. Thomas Johnson, *Relevance Regained,* The Free Press, 1992).

A leader of transformation, and managers involved, need to learn the psychology of individuals, the psychology of a group, the psychology of society, and the psychology of change.

Some understanding of variation, including appreciation of a stable system, and some understanding of special causes and common causes of variation, are essential for management of a system, including management of people (Chs. 6, 7, 8, 9, 10).

A System

What is a system? As we learned in Chapter 3, a system is a network of interdependent components that work together to try to accomplish the aim of the system. A system must have an aim. Without an aim, there is no system.

We learned also in Chapter 3 that a system must be managed.

Interdependence. The greater the interdependence between components, the greater will be the need for communication and cooperation between them. Also, the greater will be the need for overall management. Figure 9 illustrates degree of interdependence, from low to high.

Failure of management to comprehend interdependence between components is in fact the cause of loss from use of M.B.O. in practice. The efforts of the various divisions in a company, each given a job, are not additive. Their efforts are interdependent. One division, to achieve its goals, may, left to itself, kill off another division. Peter Drucker is clear on this point.[2]

An example of a system, well optimized, is a good orchestra. The players are not there to play solos as prima donnas, each one trying to catch the ear of the listener. They are there to support each other. Individually, they need not be the best players in the country.

Thus, each of the 140 players in the Royal Philharmonic Orchestra of London is there to support the other 139 players. An orchestra is judged by listeners, not so much by illustrious players, but by the way they work together. The conductor, as manager, begets cooperation between the

[2]Peter Drucker, *Management Tasks, Responsibilities, Practices* (Harper & Row, 1973).

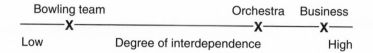

Fig. 9. Interdependence, from low to high.

players, as a system, every player to support the others. There are other aims for an orchestra, such as joy in work for the players and for the conductor.

Obligation of a component. The obligation of any component is to contribute its best to the system, not to maximize its own production, profit, or sales, nor any other competitive measure. Some components may operate at a loss to themselves in order to optimize the whole system, including the components that take a loss.

We saw in Chapter 3 an example where the travel department saved money on fares, causing heavy loss in efficiency of the traveller. Similarly, the purchasing department in a company can easily save money at first cost, but cause heavy losses downstream.

Basis for negotiation. Best for everyone concerned should be the basis for negotiation between people, between divisions, between union and management, between companies, between components, between countries. Everybody would gain.

The fruits of negotiation will be impaired if not demol-

97

ished if one party drops out of the agreement to follow a path of selfish reward.

Knowledge about Variation

Life is variation. Variation there will always be, between people, in output, in service, in product. What is the variation trying to tell us about a process, and about the people that work in it?

Need a teacher understand something about variation? Mr. Heero Hacquebord sent his six-year-old daughter to school. She came home in a few weeks with a note from the teacher with the horrible news that she had so far been given two tests, and this little girl was below average in both tests. Warning to the parents that trouble lies ahead. Other parents received the same note, and were worried. They wished to believe Mr. Hacquebord's words of comfort that such comparisons meant nothing, but they were afraid to. Other parents received notes. For example, your little boy was above average in both tests. Prepare for a genius coming up. Or, your little girl was above average on the first test, but sank to below average on the second test.

The little girl learned that she was below average in both tests. The news affected her adversely. She was humiliated, inferior. Her parents put her into a school that nourishes confidence. She recovered.

What if she had not recovered? A life lost. How many children were affected and had not the benefit of such supportive help? Nobody knows.

The teacher failed to observe that roughly half of her pupils will be above average on any test, and the other half below. Half of the people in any area will be above average for that area in test of cholesterol. There is not much that anyone can do about it.

When do data indicate that a process is stable, that the distribution of the output is predictable? Once a process has been brought into a state of statistical control, it has a definable capability. A process that is not in statistical control has not a definable capability: its performance is not predictable.

There are two mistakes frequently made in attempts to improve results, both costly (*Out of the Crisis,* p. 318). We shall study them in detail in Chapter 8.

> Mistake 1. To react to an outcome as if it came from a special cause, when actually it came from common causes of variation.

> Mistake 2. To treat an outcome as if it came from common causes of variation, when actually it came from a special cause.

Shewhart prescribed procedures aimed at minimum economic loss from the two mistakes (Ch. 8).

Stable and unstable states. A process may be in statistical control; it may not be. In the state of statistical control, the variation to expect in the future is predictable. Costs, performance, quality, and quantity are predictable. Shewhart called this the stable state. If the process is not stable, then it is unstable. Its performance is not predictable. (More in Chs. 7 and 8.)

Management of people (leader, supervisor, teacher) is entirely different in the two states, stable and unstable. Confusion between the two states leads to calamity.

Management requires knowledge about interaction of forces. Interaction may reinforce efforts, or it may nullify efforts. Management of people requires knowledge of the effect of the system on the performance of people (Ch. 6). Knowledge of dependence and interdependence between people, groups, divisions, companies, countries, is helpful.

Use of data requires knowledge about the different sources of uncertainty. Measurement is a process. Is the system of measurement stable or unstable?

Use of data requires also understanding of the distinction between enumerative studies and analytic problems. An enumerative study produces information about a frame. The theory of sampling and design of experiments are enumerative studies. Our Census is an enumerative study. Another example is a shipload of iron ore. Buyer and seller need to know how much iron is on board.

The interpretation of results of a test or experiment is something else. It is prediction that a specific change in a process or procedure will be a wise choice, or that no change would be better. Either way the choice is prediction. This is known as an analytic problem, or a problem of inference, prediction. Tests of significance, t-test, chi-square, are useless as inference—i.e., useless for aid in prediction. Test of hypothesis has been for half a century a bristling obstruction to understanding statistical inference.

> **Question in a seminar.** Please elaborate on your statement that profound knowledge comes from outside the system. Aren't the people in the system the only ones that know what is happening, and why?

> **Answer:** The people that work in any organization know what they are doing, but they will not by themselves learn a better way. Their best efforts and hard work only dig deeper the pit that they are working in. Their best efforts and hard work do not provide an outside view of the organization.

Again, a system can not understand itself. One may learn a lot about ice, yet know very little about water.

Theory of Knowledge[3]

Management is prediction. The theory of knowledge helps us to understand that management in any form is prediction. The simplest plan—how may I go home tonight—

---

[3]Clarence Irving Lewis, *Mind and the World-Order* (Scribner's, 1929). Reprinted by Dover Press, New York. My advice to a reader is start with Ch. 6, 7, or 8, not with page 1.

requires prediction that my automobile will start and run, or that the bus will come, or the train.

Knowledge is built on theory. The theory of knowledge teaches us that a statement, if it conveys knowledge, predicts future outcome, with risk of being wrong, and that it fits without failure observations of the past.

Rational prediction requires theory and builds knowledge through systematic revision and extension of theory based on comparison of prediction with observation.

> The barnyard rooster Chanticleer had a theory. He crowed every morning, putting forth all his energy, flapped his wings. The sun came up. The connexion was clear: His crowing caused the sun to come up. There was no question about his importance.
>
> There came a snag. He forgot one morning to crow. The sun came up anyhow. Crestfallen, he saw his theory in need of revision.

Without his theory, he would have had nothing to revise, nothing to learn.

> Plane Euclidean geometry served the world well for a flat earth. Every corollary and every theorem in the book is correct in its own world.
>
> Use of the theory for a flat earth fails on this earth when man extends his horizon to bigger buildings, and to roads that go beyond the village.

> Parallel lines with a north declination are not equidistant. The angles of a triangle do not add up to 180°. Spherical correction is required—a new geometry.

It is extension of application that discloses inadequacy of a theory, and need for revision, or even new theory. Again, without theory, there is nothing to revise. Without theory, experience has no meaning. Without theory, one has no questions to ask. Hence without theory, there is no learning.

Theory is a window into the world. Theory leads to prediction. Without prediction, experience and examples teach nothing. To copy an example of success, without understanding it with the aid of theory, may lead to disaster.

Any rational plan, however simple, is prediction concerning conditions, behavior, performance of people, procedures, equipment, or materials.

Use of data requires prediction. Interpretation of data from a test or experiment is prediction—what will happen on application of the conclusions or recommendations that are drawn from a test or experiment? This prediction will depend largely on knowledge of the subject matter. It is only in the state of statistical control that statistical theory provides, with a high degree of belief, prediction of performance in the immediate future.

> An example is contained in the following conclusion, based on tests of two methods, A and B. I will continue to use Method A, and not change

to Method B, because at this moment evidence that Method B will be dependably better in the future is not convincing.

A statement devoid of rational prediction does not convey knowledge.

No number of examples establishes a theory, yet a single unexplained failure of a theory requires modification or even abandonment of the theory.

No true value. There is no true value of any characteristic, state, or condition that is defined in terms of measurement or observation. Change of procedure for measurement (change in operational definition) or observation produces a new number.

There is a true value of the number of prime numbers under 100. Just write them down, and count them—2, 3, 5, 7, 11, …. This is information, not knowledge (p. 106). It predicts nothing except that anybody else would get the same number. Likewise, it is a fact—information—that the reader is reading these lines.

There is no true value of the number of people in a room. Whom do you count? Do we count someone that was here in this room, but is now outside on the telephone or drinking coffee? Do we count the people that work for the hotel? Do we count the people on the stage? the people managing the audio-visual equipment? If you change the rule for counting people, you come up with a new number.

The procedure will depend on the purpose. If our job is to prepare lunch for the people that will stay through lunch, then we need to count the people that will be here for lunch.

If the problem is the total weight of the people in this room (are we in violation of fire regulations?), then we should count everybody in the room.

There is no true value of the amount of iron in a shipload of iron ore. Why? Change of procedure for taking samples of the ore from the shipload will produce a new number for the proportion of iron in the iron ore. Repetition of any procedure will produce a new number.

How would you count the people on boats in San Diego?

There is no such thing as a fact concerning an empirical observation. Any two people may have different ideas about what is important to know about any event. Get the facts! Is there any meaning to this exhortation?

Communication and negotiation (as between customer and supplier, between management and union, between countries) require for optimization operational definitions. An operational definition is a procedure agreed upon for translation of a concept into measurement of some kind.

Operational definitions. An example. Dr. Mary Leit-naker, Professor of Statistics at the University of Tennessee at Knoxville, uses a simple exercise in her teaching of operational definitions. She goes to the grocery store and buys half a dozen packages of animal crackers, dumps them on to a table in her classroom, and asks her pupils to count the cows, horses, and pigs. Straightaway comes this question, "Is this a cow? One leg is missing. Should I count her as a cow?" Neither yes or no is correct, but the pupil needs to know the rules. Change of rule, count her as a cow, or do not, changes the count of cows.

Information is not knowledge. We are today in possession of instant communication with any part of the world. Unfortunately, speed does not help anyone to understand the future and the obligations of management. Many of us deceive ourselves into the supposition that we need constant updating to cope with the rapidly changing future. But you can not, by watching every moment of television, or by reading every newspaper, acquire a glimpse of what the future holds.

To put it another way, information, no matter how complete and speedy, is not knowledge. Knowledge has temporal spread. Knowledge comes from theory. Without theory, there is no way to use the information that comes to us on the instant.

A dictionary contains information, but not knowledge. A dictionary is useful. I use a dictionary frequently when at my desk, but the dictionary will not prepare a paragraph nor criticize it.

Losses from successive application of random impulses.
Wild results and losses may come from successive application of random forces or random changes that may individually be unimportant (exemplified in the experiment with
the funnel, Ch. 9). Examples:
1. Worker training worker in succession
2. Management of a company, or a committee in
   industry or in government, working with best
   efforts on policy, leading themselves astray
   without guidance of profound knowledge

Some important signposts for profound knowledge.
Enlargement of a committee does not necessarily improve
results. Enlargement of a committee is not a reliable way to
acquire profound knowledge.

Corollaries of this theorem are frightening. True, popular
vote acts as a ballast over a dictator, but does it provide the
right answer?

Does the House of Bishops serve the church better than
governance vested in the Archbishop? History leads to
grave doubts.

Psychology[4]

Psychology helps us to understand people, interaction
between people and circumstances, interaction between
customer and supplier, interaction between teacher and

---

[4]A number of friends have contributed to this section. I am especially
indebted to Dr. Wendy Coles and Dr. Linda Doherty.

pupil, interaction between a manager and his people and any system of management.

People are different from one another. A manager of people must be aware of these differences, and use them for optimization of everybody's abilities and inclinations. This is not ranking people. Management of industry, education, and government operate today under the supposition that all people are alike.

People learn in different ways, and at different speeds. Some learn a skill by reading, some by listening, some by watching pictures, still or moving, some by watching someone do it.

There are intrinsic sources of motivation, extrinsic sources of motivation, and the phenomenon of over-justification.

People are born with a need for relationships with other people, and need for love and esteem by others.

One is born with a natural inclination to learn. Learning is a source of innovation. One inherits a right to enjoy his work. Good management helps us to nurture and preserve these positive innate attributes of people.

Family environment may shatter at early age dignity, self-esteem, and thereby shatter also intrinsic motivation. Some practices of management (e.g., ranking people) complete the destruction (Ch. 2, Ch. 6).

Extrinsic motivation may indirectly bring positive results. For example, a man takes a job and receives money. Money is extrinsic reward. He arrives at work on time, and comes in a clean shirt, and discovers some of his abilities, all of which helps his self-esteem.

Some extrinsic motivation helps to build self-esteem. But total submission to extrinsic motivation leads to destruction of the individual, as Figure 10 in Chapter 6 exhibits. Joy in learning is submerged in order to capture top grades. On the job, under the present system, joy in work, and innovation, become secondary to a good rating. Extrinsic motivation in the extreme crushes intrinsic motivation.

A bonus for high rank in the ranking of people, teams, divisions, regions, brings demoralization to all the people concerned, including him that receives the bonus.

I repeat here Norb Keller's famous statement made on 8 November 1987 in a meeting in General Motors: "If General Motors were to double the pay of everybody commencing the first of December, performance would be exactly what it is now."

He was of course talking about pay above that needed to maintain quality of life. He also meant to include everybody, not a selected group.

> Some of his friends told him afterward that they would be willing to take part in an experiment in double pay, but they acknowledged in the same breath that double pay would make no difference in their performance.

No one, child or grown-up, can enjoy learning if he must constantly be concerned about grading and gold stars for his performance. Our educational system would be improved immeasurably by abolishment of grading. No one can enjoy his work if he will be ranked with others.

The phenomenon of overjustification. Systems of reward now in place may actually be overjustification. Monetary reward to somebody, or a prize, for an act or achievement that he did for sheer pleasure and self-satisfaction may be viewed as overjustification. The result of monetary reward under these conditions is at best meaningless and a source of discouragement. He that receives an award from someone that he does not respect will feel further degraded.

To clarify overjustification, I relate here an example told to me by Dr. Joyce Orsini.

> A little boy took it into his head for reasons unknown to wash the dishes after supper every evening. His mother was pleased with such a fine boy. One evening, to show her appreciation, she handed to him a quarter. He never washed another dish. Her payment to him changed their relationship. It hurt his dignity. He had washed the dishes for the sheer pleasure of doing something for his mother.

Further remarks on rewards.[5] When children are given rewards such as toys and money for doing well in school, music, and sports, they learn to expect rewards for good per-

[5]This section is contributed by Dr. Linda Doherty.

formance. As they become adults, their desire for tangible reward begins to govern action. They are now extrinsically motivated. They come to rely on the world to provide things to make them feel good. They will often work hard to earn lots of money, only to find in middle age that their work has no meaning. Anyone that derives meaning from extrinsic sources of motivation brings detrimental effects on his self-esteem. He feels that he has no control over the world. He is powerless, and may become despondent.

The loving mother, the kind teacher, the patient coach, can through praise, respect, and support for improvement, reenforce a child's dignity and self-esteem. Children feel good about themselves when they learn how to master a new activity. They become more intrinsically motivated. They develop self-esteem and confidence. They develop self-efficacy. Their work is meaningful, and they will make improvements in what they do.

My son Tad was on a swimming team from the time that he was 5 until 17. When the younger children were in a race, all got medals. They were very excited about the medals. The parents liked them. Important people, the coaches, gave them out. The swimmers were extrinsically motivated to swim better. As the children grew older, medals lost their importance. They found enjoyment and meaning in improvement of performance. My son knew how fast he swam. He would not even pick up the medals. He had become intrinsically motivated and developed self-discipline. The four-hour-a-day workouts, at times in the rain and cold, would have been too difficult had he not found reward in the activity. Some parents offered money or presents to their children to swim better. These children did not pursue swimming.

The most important act that a manager can take is to understand what it is that is important to an individual. Everyone is different from everyone else. All people are motivated to a different degree extrinsically and intrinsically. This is why it is so vital that managers spend time to listen to an employee to understand whether he is looking for recognition by the company, or by his peers, time at work to publish, flexible working hours, time to take a university course. In this way, a manager can provide positive outcomes for his people, and may even move some people toward replacement of extrinsic motivation with intrinsic motivation.

Examples of overjustification. A man, not an employee of the hotel, picked up my bag at the registration desk of a hotel in Detroit, carried it to my room. The bag was heavy. I was exhausted and hungry, hoping to get into the dining room before it would close at 11 p.m. I was ever so grateful to him; fished out two dollar bills for him. He refused them. I had hurt his feelings, trying to offer money to him. He had carried the bag for me, not for pay. My attempt to pay him was, in effect, an attempt to change our relationship. I meant well, but did the wrong thing. I resolved to be careful.

And then I did it again. As I arrived via U.S. Air at

National Airport, Washington, a member of the crew picked up my bag (heavy), carried it off the aeroplane, escorted me with the other hand through the airport, down and out to my driver waiting for me. Grateful, I hurriedly found a five-dollar bill and pushed it toward her. "Oh, no." I had done it again! Stupefied, I asked her name. Debbie. I wrote to the president of the airline to ask for Debbie's full name and address, so that I could apologize to her. He replied that he had several Debbies in Washington, and could not be sure which one assisted me.

I wonder how many times I have made this same mistake.

An award in the form of money for a job done for the sheer pleasure of doing it is demoralizing, overjustification. Merit awards and ranking are demoralizing. They generate conflict and dissatisfaction. Companies with wrong practices pay a penalty. The penalty can not be measured.

Rewards motivate people to work for rewards.[6]

Appreciation? Certainly. A show of appreciation to someone may mean far more to him than monetary reward.

A physician, Dr. Dv, immunologist, prescribed vaccine for me when I was in the hospital with an infected leg. He sent to me, in due time, a bill. Along with the cheque to him, I enclosed a brief note of thanks and appreciation for his knowledge and for the care that he showed to me. I encountered him by chance one day, weeks later. The

[6]Alfie Kohn, Cincinnati, 11 August 1992.

cheque we had both forgotten, but the letter? No. He had it in his pocket. It meant a lot to him, he told me, to know that someone cared.

Two years later, when I went to see Dr. Sh in Washington, he remarked to me in passing, "I ran across Dr. Dv the other day: he asked about you."

What if I had added five dollars to the Dr. Dv cheque in appreciation? That would have wounded him. That would have been a horrible example of overjustification.

A good plan of appreciation, I submit, would be to donate a sum of money to a hospital to be dispensed under the guidance of Dr. Dv for medical care for patients that can not pay.

Question in a seminar. If management does not reward employees for a good job, people will move to a company that is willing to reward them. Some people go where they can get more money.

Answer: Everyone that I work with could get higher pay in some other company. Why does he stay here? He stays here because he likes it here. He has a chance to use his knowledge for the benefit of the whole system. He takes joy in his work. Money, above a certain level, is not enticement. Money may entice someone that knows that he is inferior. Certainly a boss should give a pat on the back for a job well done.

Many managers of people understand that the current methods of rating people do not distinguish the contribution of the individual from the rest of the process, yet they hold on to the belief or hope that a method of appraisal could be developed that would do so.

It is easy to miss the point that even if a method were developed to rank people with precision and certainty, distinct from the process that they work in, why would anyone suppose that this would improve people or the process? (This is a further contribution from Mr. Norb Keller of General Motors on 8 November 1987.)

5

Leadership

You can not plan to make a discovery.—Irving Langmuir

Aim of this chapter. Understanding of profound knowledge will lead to transformation of management. The transformation will lead to adoption of what we have learned to call a system, with a stated aim. The individual components of the system, instead of being competitive, will for optimization reenforce each other. The same transformation is required in government and education.

Transformation in any organization will take place under a leader. It will not be spontaneous. We therefore devote some space here to the subject of leadership.

What is a leader? As I use the term here, the job of a leader is to accomplish transformation of his organization. He possesses knowledge, personality, and persuasive power (Ch. 6).

How may he accomplish transformation? First, he has theory. He understands why the transformation would bring gains to his organization and to all the people that his organization deals with. Second, he feels compelled to accomplish the transformation as an obligation to himself and to his organization. Third, he is a practical man. He has a plan, step by step, and can explain it in simple terms.

But what is in his own head is not enough. He must convince and change enough people in power to make it happen. He possesses persuasive power. He understands people.

Great ideas: great plans. People with great ideas suffer much frustration, if I may say so on the basis of letters that come to me every week. Somebody has a great idea, so great that I can not understand it. His distress comes from the fact that his boss has no interest in talking about the great idea. Even his colleagues do not wax enthusiastic about it. The great idea merely bounces back; goes nowhere. I may offer the suggestion that the presentation must describe a plan of action, with prediction of results. Acceptance and action on a great idea depend on simplicity and brevity in presentation.

Example of a leader. An example may help to explain my use of the word *leader*. There have been many leaders in history, some for good, some for evil. My friend Morris H. Hansen, who died on 9 October 1990, at age 79, provides an example of a leader great and good.

The country was in the 1930s in a deep depression, set off by the crash of the stock market in 1929. Unemployment in the 1930s was pitiful, though an operational definition of unemployed had not yet been formulated. The term used was gainful worker, someone that earned money.

Meanwhile, each of a number of experts made his own estimate of people not gainful workers. These estimates were so wide apart that they were all discarded.

Congress, frustrated with wild estimates, ordered a census of people not gainfully employed. Every mail carrier in the country would obtain from everyone on his route information about employment. The Post Office Department in Washington had a complete list of mail carriers. All very simple, so it seemed. The Federal Emergency Relief Administration was charged with the responsibility to carry out the order. Mr. John B. Biggers, then President of Libby-Owens-Ford Glass Company, was recruited to take charge. The Biggers study it became. The results went into a large volume, predictably useless.

Morris H. Hansen, then at age 24, had found in 1935 a job as a statistical clerk in the Bureau of the Census in Washington. He had studied with Professor Forest Hall at the University of Wyoming, and upon arrival in Washington, took courses in statistical theory at American University, where he earned a master's degree. He was thus in possession of some knowledge of the theory of probability, and of errors in surveys. He contrived a plan for selection by random numbers 52 of the postal routes for special treatment, such as thoroughness of coverage, and investigation into the meaning of the answers to questions about gainful workers.

The results of Hansen's sample of postal routes, published in a small volume, were accepted by Congress. The Biggers study, the complete census, was ignored, afflicted with too many errors of nonresponse and wrong responses.

Morris Hansen was a leader. He had in his head some theory of probability along with practical sense for design of a sample of postal routes to acquire the necessary information. Further, he could explain his plan.

He could not by himself have made it happen. He convinced enough men in power that were willing and able to understand his theory. Names (undoubtedly incomplete):

Dr. Philip M. Hauser
Dr. Calvert L. Dedrick, Chief Statistician in the
    Bureau of the Census
Frederick F. Stephan, Consultant
Dr. Samuel A. Stouffer, Professor of Sociology,
    University of Wisconsin, Consultant
John Webb, in charge of operations

Incidentally, Hansen's sample of postal workers was possibly a violation of the law, as Congress had specified that the study should be complete, every household; this is a time for accuracy.

Further contributions from this study of postal routes were concepts and operational definitions of the labor force, and of unemployment and partial employment.[1]

Statistical methods for surveys took hold. The WPA (Works Progress Administration) commenced a quarterly (later monthly) survey of unemployment, under the guidance of J. Stevens Stock and Lester Frankel. This survey

[1]I am indebted to Philip M. Hauser for refreshing my memory on most of the details of this account.

was taken over in 1940 by the Bureau of the Census. Monthly and quarterly surveys of prices for the cost of living emerged, and for housing starts, all guided by the theory of probability.

The new Director of the Census, Mr. J. C. Capt, a political appointment, had taken office in 1940. He possessed uncanny sense for recognition of genuine ability. He put his power behind leaders—Morris Hansen, Philip M. Hauser, by then Assistant Director, Frederick Stephan and Samuel Stouffer as consultants. Mr. Capt had freedom to act."Only the President can remove me," he said to me.

The main part of the information about individuals and households in the U.S. Census of 1940 was collected by sampling—on the average 1 individual in 20, 1 household in 20. Sampling increased the accuracy of results, and saved much time and money in tabulation.

Before long, people came from government offices the world over to study with Morris Hansen. A division for reception and guidance of visitors was created, Dr. Calvert L. Dedrick as head.

Morris Hansen, assisted by William N. Hurwitz, ascended in knowledge and stature, to become in 1945 Assistant Director for Statistical Standards in the Bureau of the Census.

The dotted line relationships shown on page 467 of the book *Out of the Crisis* duplicates Morris Hansen's plan for the Census, a statistician in every division—Population, Agriculture, Government, Vital Statistics, Geography— with a dotted line in relationship to him.

6

Management of People

If you can not argue with your boss, he is not worth working for.—Lt. General Leslie E. Simon, U.S.A., stated in 1936 when he held the rank of Captain.

Aim of this chapter. We are living in prison, under tyranny of the prevailing style of interaction between people, between teams, between divisions. We need to throw overboard our theories and practices of the present, and build afresh. We must throw overboard the idea that competition is a necessary way of life. In place of competition, we need cooperation. The aim of this chapter is to examine ways to manage people under the new philosophy.

Effects of the present style of reward. The accompanying diagram (Fig. 10) shows some of the forces of destruction that come from the present style of reward, and their effects. What they do is to squeeze out from an individual, over his lifetime, his innate intrinsic motivation, self-esteem, dignity. They build into him fear, self-defense, extrinsic motivation. We have been destroying our people, from toddlers on through the university, and on the job. We must preserve the power of intrinsic motivation, dignity, cooperation, curiosity, joy in learning, that people are born with. The transformation set forth in this book will year by year build up the bottom half of the diagram, and shrink the upper half.

121

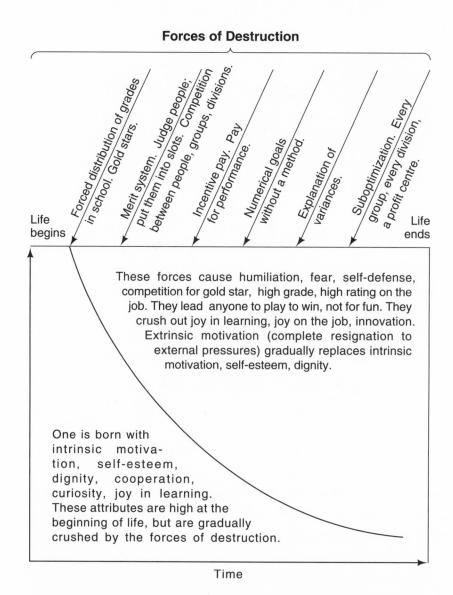

Forces of Destruction

These forces cause humiliation, fear, self-defense, competition for gold star, high grade, high rating on the job. They lead anyone to play to win, not for fun. They crush out joy in learning, joy on the job, innovation. Extrinsic motivation (complete resignation to external pressures) gradually replaces intrinsic motivation, self-esteem, dignity.

One is born with intrinsic motivation, self-esteem, dignity, cooperation, curiosity, joy in learning. These attributes are high at the beginning of life, but are gradually crushed by the forces of destruction.

Fig. 10. The forces along the top rob people, and the nation, of innovation and applied science. We must replace these forces with management that will restore the power of the individual.

122

Transformation is required in government, industry, education. Management is in a stable state. Transformation is required to move out of the present state, not mere patchwork on the present style of management. We must of course solve problems and stamp out fires as they occur, but these activities do not change the process.

The transformation will take us into a new method of reward. We must restore the individual, and do so in the complexities of interaction with the rest of the world. The transformation will release the power of human resource contained in intrinsic motivation. In place of competition for high rating, high grades, to be Number One, there will be cooperation on problems of common interest between people, divisions, companies, competitors, governments, countries. The result will in time be greater innovation, applied science, technology, expansion of market, greater service, greater material reward for everyone. There will be joy in work, joy in learning. Anyone that enjoys his work is a pleasure to work with. Everyone will win; no losers.

The function of government should be to work with business, not to harass business.

Pictorial effect of transformation. Figure 11 shows the decline that we attribute to the present style of management, and the dream of what we could be once the transformation is accomplished. The route to transformation is to understand and apply profound knowledge.

It will not suffice to learn all about the present style of management. One could learn all there is to know about

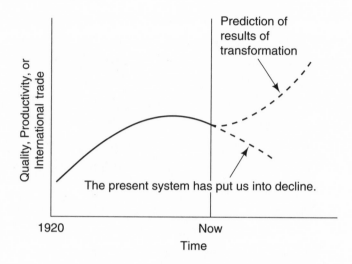

Fig. 11. Predicted effect of transformation.

ice, yet know very little about water. (Contributed by Dr. Edward M. Baker.)

Example of incompatible hopes. A corporation published this:

GOALS AND OBJECTIVES

1. Provide systems of reward that recognize superior performance, innovation, extraordinary care and commitment.

2. Create and maintain stimulating and enjoyable work environment, with the aim to attract, develop, and retain self-directed, talented people.

Comment. These two goals are incompatible. Goal 1 will induce conflict and competition between people, a sure road to demoralization. It will take the joy out of work, and will thus defeat Goal 2, however noble it be.

Management of people. In place of judgment of people, ranking them, putting them into slots (outstanding, excellent, on down to unsatisfactory), the aim should be to help people to optimize the system so that everybody will gain.

Role of a Manager of People

This is the new role of a manager of people after transformation.

1.   A manager understands and conveys to his people the meaning of a system. He explains the aims of the system. He teaches his people to understand how the work of the group supports these aims.

2.   He helps his people to see themselves as components in a system, to work in cooperation with preceding stages and with following stages toward optimization of the efforts of all stages toward achievement of the aim.

3.   A manager of people understands that people are different from each other. He tries to create for everybody interest and challenge, and joy in work. He tries to optimize the family background, education, skills, hopes, and abilities of everyone.

This is not ranking people. It is, instead, recognition of differences between people, and an attempt to put everybody in position for development.

4. He is an unceasing learner. He encourages his people to study. He provides, when possible and feasible, seminars and courses for advancement of learning. He encourages continued education in college or university for people that are so inclined.

5. He is coach and counsel, not a judge.

6. He understands a stable system. He understands the interaction between people and the circumstances that they work in. He understands that the performance of anyone that can learn a skill will come to a stable state—upon which further lessons will not bring improvement of performance. A manager of people knows that in this stable state it is distracting to tell the worker about a mistake.

7. He has three sources of power:
    1. Authority of office
    2. Knowledge
    3. Personality and persuasive power; tact

A successful manager of people develops Nos. 2 and 3; he does not rely on No. 1. He has nevertheless obligation to use No. 1, as this source of power enables him to change the process — equipment, materials, methods — to bring improvement, such as to reduce variation in output. (Dr. Robert Klekamp.)

He in authority, but lacking knowledge or personality (No. 2 or 3), must depend on his formal
power (No. 1). He unconsciously fills a void in his
qualifications by making it clear to everybody
that he is in position of authority. His will be done.

8.   He will study results with the aim to improve his performance as a manager of people.

9.   He will try to discover who if anybody is outside the
system, in need of special help. This can be accomplished
with simple calculations, if there be individual figures on
production or on failures. Special help may be only simple
rearrangement of work. It might be more complicated. He
in need of special help is not in the bottom 5 per cent of the
distribution of others: he is clean outside that distribution
(Fig. 12.).

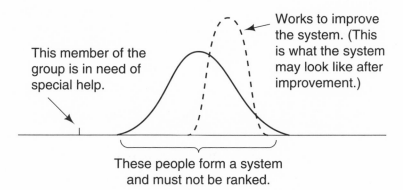

Fig. 12. Figures on production or on failures, if they
exist, can be plotted. Study of the figures will show the
system, and outliers if any.

10. He creates trust. He creates an environment that encourages freedom and innovation.

11. He does not expect perfection.

12. He listens and learns without passing judgment on him that he listens to.

13. He will hold an informal, unhurried conversation with every one of his people at least once a year, not for judgment, merely to listen. The purpose would be development of understanding of his people, their aims, hopes, and fears. The meeting will be spontaneous, not planned ahead.

14. He understands the benefits of cooperation and the losses from competition between people and between groups.[1]

More suggestions appear on pages 117 and 118 of *Out of the Crisis*.

Example. On arrival at the Nashua Tape Company in the area of Albany, New York, I saw in the conference room a number of men working with deep concern. The problem? Rejection of a roll of paper (weight one ton) at the end of the line, ready to be slit, a catastrophic loss. The men were working on the process, trying to improve it so that this catastrophe could not happen again.

On a previous similar catastrophe, a few years earlier, the procedure was very different. The superintendent of the operation pinned the blame on to some unfortunate man.

[1] Alfie Kohn, *No Contest: The Case Against Competition* (Houghton Mifflin, 1986).

Punishment: (1) censure, disgrace, the cause of the problem; (2) no more overtime for him; (3) job changed to dirtier work.

The difference between the two ways to handle the catastrophe was striking. What happened between the two events that could cause such a difference? The answer lay in the new manager, by name, Mr. Bob Geiger, and the change that he wrought in the management of people. One of his first remarks to me when I first met him was rebuke of his management for paying to him a bonus. "If they have to pay to me a bonus to make sure that I do my job, I ought not to have this job in the first place."

On their honour, it paid. The manager of a company prescribed strict rules for absence of three days to attend a funeral and family affairs for the death of a near relative. He defined with care a near relative. An employee might even be required to produce a death certificate. Saturday and Sunday and a holiday are counted in the three days. Result: every employee took all three days at every bereavement.

Then came somehow a change of heart. Let the employee make arrangements with his supervisor for absence. Result: days off for bereavement dropped to half. (Related to me by Dr. Brian L. Joiner.)

Is the company hampering itself by mismanagement of people? Suppose that the symbols A, B, C, etc., represent the separate abilities of the people in a company. What benefit does the company receive from its people? The full capability of the people in the company, working together, working with and for each other, may be expressed as:

Individuals $A + B + C + D + \cdots$

$$
\text{Interactions} \left\{
\begin{array}{l}
+ \text{ (AB)} + \text{(AC)} + \text{(AD)} + \cdots \\[4pt]
\qquad\qquad + \text{(BC)} + \text{(BD)} + \cdots \\[4pt]
\qquad\qquad\qquad\qquad + \text{(CD)} + \cdots \\[4pt]
+ \text{(ABC)} + \text{(ABD)} + \text{(BCD)} + \cdots \\[4pt]
+ \text{(ABCD)} + \cdots
\end{array}
\right.
$$

The top line is the sum of the individual abilities of the people in a company. Parentheses denote interaction between people, helping or hurting each other in pairs, triplets, etc., in teams, platforms, chimneys, divisions, departments. An interaction may be:

> Negative
> Zero
> Positive

Why is it that a company as a whole may be less than the sum of the individual abilities $A + B + C + D + \cdots$?

One possible answer is that failure of managers to make the best use of the diverse abilities, capabilities, family backgrounds, experience, and hopes of employees detracts from the possible contribution $A + B + C + D + \cdots$ in the top line.

130

Another reason could be negative interactions. Why does the company hamper itself with negative interactions? What causes them? One cause may be the merit system, ranking people, ranking salesmen, fostering competitive measures between people, teams, platforms, departments, divisions. In other words, competition.

One of management's main responsibilities is to know about the existence of interactions, to perceive how they originate, then to change negative and zero interactions into positive interactions.

Why is it that someone that leaves our company to go to another one contributes more to the new company than he contributed to ours?

The answer lies in the management of people or rather, the mismanagement of people, by which the people in the company do not work together as a system. (This paragraph is attributable to remarks made to me by Mr. Louis Lataif, then with the Ford Motor Company, now Dean of the School of Business at Boston University.)

Is your automobile as good as the parts that it is made of?

The PDSA Cycle.[2]   This cycle (Fig. 13) is a flow diagram for learning, and for improvement of a product or of a process.

Step 1.   PLAN.   Somebody has an idea for improvement of a product or of a process. This is the 0-th stage,

---

[2]The PDSA Cycle originated in my teaching in Japan in 1950. It appeared in the booklet *Elementary Principles of the Statistical Control of Quality* (JUSE, 1950; out of print).

The Shewhart Cycle for Learning and Improvement
The P D S A Cycle

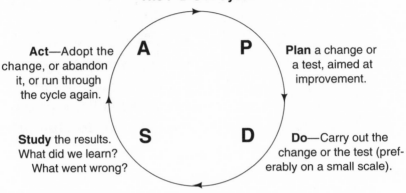

Act—Adopt the change, or abandon it, or run through the cycle again.

A

P

Plan a change or a test, aimed at improvement.

Study the results. What did we learn? What went wrong?

S

D

Do—Carry out the change or the test (preferably on a small scale).

Fig. 13. A flow diagram for learning and for improvement of a product or of a process.

embedded in Step 1. It leads to a plan for a test, comparison, experiment. Step 1 is the foundation of the whole
cycle. A hasty start may be ineffective, costly, and frustrat-
ing. People have a weakness to short-circuit this step. They
can not wait to get into motion, to be active, to look busy,
move into Step 2.

The planning stage may start with a choice between several suggestions. Which one can we test? What may be the
result? Compare the possible outcomes of the possible
choices. Of the several suggestions, which one appears to
be most promising in terms of new knowledge or profit?
The problem may be how to achieve a feasible goal.

Step 2.   DO. Carry out the test, comparison, or experiment, preferably on a small scale, according to the layout decided in Step 1.

Step 3.   STUDY. Study the results. Do they correspond with hopes and expectations? If not, what went wrong? Maybe we tricked ourselves in the first place, and should make a fresh start.

Step 4.   ACT.   Adopt the change.
        or   Abandon it.
        or   Run through the cycle again,
                 possibly under different environmental conditions, different materials, different people, different rules.

The reader may note that to adopt the change, or to abandon it, requires prediction.

Planning for a new engine. Engineers were at work on plans for a new engine. They had worked on most of the pieces of the development, but had not put the pieces in sequence. For example, they were training 100 skilled workers for machining, inspection, assembly. A flow diagram put the pieces in sequence, and showed relationships between them. Figure 14 shows the flow diagram that we arrived at just as I drew it on plastic on the overhead projector. Results of the last stage may indicate reconsidera-

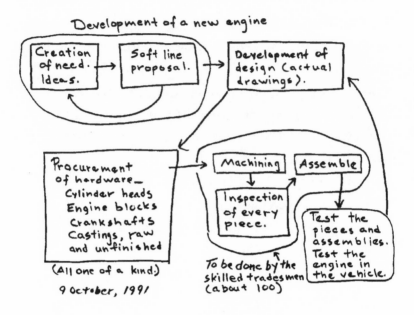

Fig. 14. Stages proposed in the development of a new engine.

tion of the stage of actual drawings. With the flow diagram in view, everyone may understand the relationships between stages.

To shorten the time of development. There is much talk about need to speed up development of a new product. The reasons given flirt around the alleged need to put a product into the hands of customers while they still have the same preferences as they say that they have today. The effort is noble but for the wrong reason. The customer will name a preference today, buy something else tomorrow. The drive for reduction in time for development of a new product, or of a method to produce cheaper and faster an existing product, is important mainly for reduction of cost.

The usual method is to rush through the development, only to find at the end that the pieces do not fit together, or that new and brilliant ideas for design have meanwhile emerged. The whole play then starts afresh with Stage 1. Time is lost; costs go up; the end product falls short of expectations.

One reason to shorten the development of a method by which to make something is to move into an existing market for a product or service that is already well established, or will be. Speed in development of the process captures profit at the point where profit is easiest to capture. This track may be far more profitable than development of a new product or service. Examples: the video recorder, FAX, the CD player. Americans invented the video recorder and FAX, the Dutch invented the CD player, but all three have become Japanese products.

The moral of the story is clear. He that can make a product cheaper can take it away from the inventor. The course for America that was right in 1960—development of new products—may not now be right.[3]

---

[3]Taken from *Harper's Magazine,* March 1992, p. 16, which in turn is taken from Lester C. Thurow, *Head to Head, The Coming Economic Battles Between Japan, Europe, and America* (William Morrow, 1992).

The secret for reduction in time of development is to put more effort into the early stages, and to study the interaction between stages. Each stage should have the benefit of more effort than the next stage.

We content ourselves here to adopt a constant ratio of cost from one stage to the next. Specifically, let the cost of any stage be $1 - x$ times the cost of the preceding stage. Then if K be the cost of the opening stage (the 0-th stage, concepts and proposals), then the cost of the n-th stage would be

$$K_n = K (1 - x)^n \tag{1}$$

The total cost through the n-th stage would be

$$T_n = K [1 + (1 - x) + (1 - x)^2 + (1 - x)^3 + \cdots + (1 - x)^n] \tag{2}$$

We note that the series in the brackets is merely $1/x$ expanded in powers of $1 - x$. This is easily seen by writing $x = 1 - (1 - x)$. This series will converge if $0 < x \leq 1$, which satisfies our requirements. Further,

$$T_n = K \left\{ [1 + (1 - x) + (1 - x)^2 + (1 - x)^3 + \cdots \text{ to infinity}] \right.$$

$$\left. - \frac{(1 - x)^{n+1}}{x} \right\}$$

$$= \frac{K}{x} [1 - (1 - x)^{n+1}] \tag{3}$$

Figure 15 shows graphically the decrease in cost and effort, stage by stage, in the sequence of development of a process or of a product.

For a numerical illustration, not as a recommendation, we set $x = 0.2$. Then the cost of 8 stages beyond the 0-th stage will be

$$T_8 = \frac{K}{0.2}\left[1 - (1 - 0.2)^9\right]$$

$$= 5\,K\left[1 - 0.1342\right]$$

$$= 4.33\,K \qquad\qquad (4)$$

The average cost per stage of all 9 stages (counting the 0-th stage) would be 0.481 times the cost of the 0-th stage.

The cost of the 8-th stage beyond the 0-th stage would be only $0.168\,K$, or about 1/6th the cost of the 0-th stage.

The 0-th stage is the foundation for the whole project. The 0-th stage is the place for ideas and brainstorming, to avoid so far as possible changes in direction and backtracking in later stages. Changes in direction cost more and more with each stage.

It is impossible to eliminate backtracking entirely, but under the scheme proposed here, backtracking will be reduced and will be more effective, the whole development speedier, with reduction of total cost.

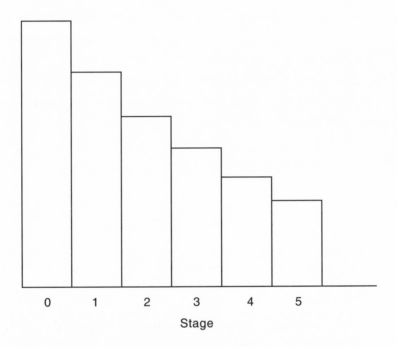

Fig. 15. Graphical display of the decrease in cost and effort, stage by stage, highest at the 0-th stage—ideas, concepts, imagination. The sequence is drawn as a geometric series, the cost of any stage being only $1 - x$ times the cost of the preceding stage.

The job of the program manager is to manage all the interfaces, to manage the system as a whole, not to optimize any stage.

Each stage may have a leader, but everyone involved might well work in all stages. A marketing man might well be a member of the team, especially at the 0-th stage.

Suppliers and toolmakers should be chosen at the 0-th stage, and made members of the team. They will be ready and waiting with supplies and tools when development of the product reaches the last stage. They will contribute to every stage, including the 0-th stage.

The manager of the whole vehicle must be a member of the team for development of an engine.

It will be necessary for top management to block the privilege of anybody in top management or in any other level to come along at the end of the line with a bright idea. A bright idea belongs in the 0-th stage, not in the last stage.

The system of development must be managed. It will not manage itself.

Example. As I understand it, the manager of Ford's maker of transmissions at Batavia increased effort and cost on the initial stage, with the aim to improve the uniformity of castings before work was done on them. Results: this increase of effort at the start cut the cost of transmissions to half, and improved greatly the quality of the end product.

A word on current accounting practice in development. Costs associated with capital equipment for a new product or process will also follow a geometric decay, $1 - x$ in successive stages, even though traditional accounting practice will show the expense to be in the future.

Current accounting practice reenforces the incorrect perception that decisions made during development are independent of future costs. One should remember that future costs include capital expenditures plus maintenance, operations, and losses suffered by customers.

Danger in divided responsibility.[4] I was working with a client. This means work through breakfast; then a meeting an hour and a half here, two hours in another meeting there, and so on; work through dinner. Came two people from the payroll department of a division of 900 people, desperate for help. What is the problem? I asked. Answer: We try to pay everyone on Thursday after the close of the preceding week. To accomplish this aim, we work overtime, nights, Saturdays. We work harder and harder, but fall further and further behind. Working at what? I asked. Answer: Those payroll cards; many of them are inconsistent; many are obviously in error; entries omitted. Let me see the card (Fig. 16).

The reader will perceive at once the source of the problem—two signatures. The worker signs the card, leaving the foreman to correct the mistakes. The foreman signs it under the supposition that the worker should know better than anyone what he did. Result: omissions, inconsistencies, and wrong entries.

Solution: Cross out the foreman's space on the 900 cards that you will use next week; same for the 900 cards for the following week. By then, you can have new cards with no space for the foreman. Further, if a worker could

---

[4]Taken from *Out of the Crisis* (MIT, CAES, 1986), pp. 208–209.

Date _____   _____   _____
         Day   Month   Year

_____   _____
Identification number   Signature

| Clock | | Elapsed time | Job code | Pay code | Amount earned |
In	Out				
Total earned this day					

_____
                Foreman

Fig. 16. Payroll time card. Too many signatures. Too much arithmetic for the employee.

have filled out the card correctly—be sure that he could—return the card to him. You don't need to stamp a message on it to say that his pay may be delayed. He will understand this without help. The problem will vanish in three weeks.

Three weeks? The problem disappeared in one week. What happened? By Monday afternoon, a dozen of the 900 people received their cards, returned. By Tuesday noon, another 25 cards were returned. All 900 people knew by Tuesday noon that if you fail to fill out your payroll card correctly, it will come back to you and your pay may be delayed. The problem disappeared in one week.

The secret? Simple. If the worker can fill out his card correctly, expect him to do it—let him do it. Do not take his job away from by him sharing it with his foreman. With shared responsibility, no one is responsible.

Joint responsibility. Joint responsibility is totally different from divided responsibility. Many of anybody's activities involve joint responsibility. An example is teacher and pupil. Learning under a teacher is a joint effort between teacher and pupil. Anyone that works in an organization works jointly, or should, with his suppliers and customers. Two people that sign a note are jointly responsible for payment: either or both together are liable for payment. Marriage creates joint responsibility. Membership on a committee is joint responsibility with the other members: each member is responsible for the recommendations of the committee.

Promotion. Promotion is movement into a new job, movement from one job to a different job. There is no way to predict with a high degree of belief that someone selected for promotion will do well in the new job.

The usual method for selection of someone for promotion is by recommendation. One's chance for promotion depends on who knows him—or put another way, who knows you?

He that recommends someone for promotion is on his honour. He has, so he thinks, good reason to believe that the candidate that he recommends will do well in the new job. Such a state of belief does not come suddenly. It comes from intimate knowledge of the candidate's performance over a long period of time, 15 years or more.

Performance in a job held at present, even if we could evaluate performance in it, would not be a basis for prediction of performance in a new job.

What ought a school of business teach? Schools of business teach how business is conducted at present. In other words, they teach perpetuation of the present style of management. They teach perpetuation of our decline.

A school of business has obligation to prepare students to lead the transformation, to halt our decline and turn it upward. They ought to teach the theory of a system and the theory of profound knowledge for transformation. They ought to teach the damage, unmeasurable, that comes from:

> The evils of short-term thinking
> Ranking people, teams, plants, divisions, with

143

     reward at the top, punishment at the bottom
     The evils of the merit system
     Losses from management by results, tampering
     Demoralization and losses from incentive pay
         and from pay for performance (for the simple
         reason that performance can not be measured)

Profound knowledge tells us why these practices cause loss and damage to people.

Students in a school of business should study also, of course, economics, statistical theory, some language (at least two years), some science (at least two years).

In desperation on what to teach, two schools of business (namely, the Stern School of Business of New York University, and the Graduate School of Business of Columbia University) ask for suggestions from students. These questions go to students toward the end of a semester:

   1. Which readings and texts did you find to be
      a. of most value to you personally?
      b. of least value?
   2. Which topics were important enough to warrant more time next year?
   3. Which topics would warrant less time next year?
   4. Which other topics should be included?

How could a student know what to teach? He may have ideas worth listening to 10 or 15 years from now.

A remark on education.   There is deep concern in the United States today about education. No notable improvement will come until our schools:

- Abolish grades (A, B, C, D) in school, from toddlers on up through the university. When graded, pupils put emphasis on the grade, not on learning. Cooperation on a project in school may be considered cheating (W. W. Scherkenbach, *The Deming Route*, p. 128). The greatest evil from grades is forced ranking—only (e.g.) 20 per cent of pupils may receive A. Ridiculous. There is no shortage of good pupils.
- Abolish merit ratings for teachers.
- Abolish comparison of schools on the basis of scores.
- Abolish gold stars for athletics or for best costume.

Indeed, if our future lies in specialty products and services, as mass production moves to automation and to other countries, then improvement of education in this country is even more vital than hitherto supposed. We must from now on live by services that bring money into the country, and by high-value, high-profit machines and apparatus.

Our schools must preserve and nurture the yearning for learning that everyone is born with (see p. 121).

Joy in learning comes not so much from what is learned, but from learning.

Joy on the job comes not so much from the result, the product, but from contribution to optimization of the system in which everybody wins.

Against grading in school. A grade is only somebody's (e.g., teacher's) assessment of a pupil's achievement on some arbitrary scale. Does the scale make any sense? Will high achievement on this scale predict future performance of the pupil in business, government, education, or as a teacher? Some other scale might be a better predictor. Some other pupil, low on the prescribed scale, might perform better in the future than the one that made a high grade on it.

A grade given to a student is nevertheless used as prediction that he will in the future do well, or do badly. A grade is a permanent label. A grade opens doors; it closes doors. How may a teacher know how someone will do in the future? If a student seems to lag behind other members of the class, it may be the fault of the teaching. He may excel all the others in some attribute not tested.

How does a student get a good grade? By feeding back to the teacher the same marbles that the teacher gave out to the class (so stated by Dr. Edward Rothman, 1990).

Grading in school is an attempt to achieve quality by inspection (William J. Latzko).

The evils of grading are intensified by forced ranking, only so many in Grade A permitted (see the next heading).

Because of such folly, I do not give grades to my students.

146

They all pass. I read the papers that my students turn in, not to grade them, but:

> To learn how I as a teacher am doing. In what ways am I failing? How can I improve my teaching?
>
> To discover whether any student is in need of special help, and to see that he gets it.
>
> To discover whether any student is extra well prepared and could receive benefit from extra work. For one such student I suggested the study of the theory of extreme values. She was fascinated with the study. So was I.

Students may take their time; do not rush a paper to me. Some of the best papers have come to me a year late. Meanwhile, the student has his grade, P for Pass.

Ranking and grading produce artificial scarcity.[5] If two people play tennis, one wins, one loses. The same for poker, swimming match, high jump, horse race. The human race has enjoyed games for centuries. The Greeks had their Olympic games and so do we. There is no harm in a game, and no sin in winning a game, so far as I know.

There is scarcity of winners in a game. Only one player can come out on top. The human race has somehow, for reasons unknown, carried the pattern of games into grades in school and on up through the university, gold stars for school athletics, the merit system (putting people into slots), ranking groups and divisions within the company.

---

[5]Alfie Kohn, *No Contest* (Houghton Mifflin, 1986).

All these practices induce competition between people.

Grading and ranking produce artificial scarcity of top grades. Only a few students are admitted to the top grades (see table below). Only a few people on the job are admitted to top rank.

This is wrong. There is no scarcity of good pupils. There is no scarcity of good people. There is no reason why everyone in a class should not be in the top grade, nor at the bottom, nor anywhere else. Moreover, a grade is only the teacher's subjective opinion. This is so even for the result of an examination.

What is the effect of grading and ranking? Answer: humiliation of those that do not receive top grades or top rank. The effect of humiliation is demoralization of the individual. Even he that receives top grades or top rank is demoralized.

I may cite as a horrible example a recommendation of a Department of Statistics, dated October 1991:

Grade	Percentage
A	20
B	30
C	30
D	20
Total	100

Of all people that should know better, it should be teachers of statistics, and certainly in a school of business. They should teach why forced ranking is wrong.

Theory of a system, win, win, needed in education. Our children go to school, learn history, something about the English language. They do not learn that the word *man* has two meanings, the masculine gender, a man, and the neuter man, mankind, as in chairman, spokesman, tradesman, salesman. They learn something about geography (not as a study in economics, but cluttered with information such as the names of the capital cities of the 50 states). Geography if taught as economics, history, sociology, anthropology could be interesting and could impart knowledge (not mere information). For example, Minneapolis is in place because it is head of navigation. Likewise for Washington, and for Albany and Schenectady. Halifax, Quebec, Montreal, and Winnipeg are in place for good reasons, not by accident.

Also missing in school is the teaching of civic responsibilities in the form of a system for win, win. Instead, students come through school with the thought that everything is competition, that there must be winners, there must be losers. One must strive to be a winner; that anyone should vote for the candidate that promises the most for the voter's hometown, not understanding that this course will lead to win, lose; that everyone will lose.

Some examples of effects of grading, gold stars, prizes.
1. Letter from a woman that attended my four-day seminar:

You spoke of the damage that we do to our children by grading them and fostering competition. I remember my son in first grade, now a freshman at Florida State University. He attended a small private school in New Orleans. The school had an annual science fair. Students in grades six and above were required to enter a project; students in the lower grades could enter if they chose to. My son decided in the first grade to enter a project. He planned and worked on it all by himself. He took it to school the morning of the fair. He was proud of his accomplishment, and excited about seeing his project on display. We went to the school that night to see it. Some projects had prize ribbons pinned on them. His did not. Some projects had won, and his had lost. He never entered another science project until required to do so in the sixth grade.

2. A letter from two of my students, written in cooperation:

Alfie Kohn, in his book, *No Contest: The Case Against Competition,* challenges the assumption that competition is necessary, productive, beneficial. He disputes four widely held myths regarding competition:

　　1. That it is an inevitable part of human nature
　　2. That it is more productive than cooperation in promoting success

150

3. That competition is more enjoyable
4. That it builds character

He then goes on to assert and defend the converse of each of these myths.

The aim of a class in gymnasium should be physical benefit to everybody. Instead, gym classes were typically spent playing a competitive game. The child that did not display athletic ability received no benefit from gymnasium. For example, in softball, the nonathletic child would be placed in right field, where the ball would seldom be hit; in basketball, she would sit on the bench till her team had a substantial lead, and be sent in when she could not jeopardize victory. Thus, from a very early age, once the child is labeled nonathletic, there is little opportunity for benefit from gym classes.

Even the method for forming teams involved a contest, winners and losers. The gym teacher would select captains, who would then choose their teams. The captains selected the best players first, and then with consultation of these players, selected the next level of players. The last to be picked would endure the humiliating experience of being judged by their peers as inferior.

In the classroom, we had a chance to shine. However, others did not. Students were early labeled winners and losers. This stifled natural motivation and joy of learning. The classroom version of the benchwarmer was afraid to raise his hand for fear of giving the wrong answer and being laughed at. Emphasis on being right discourages students from trying, and also teaches an inaccurate lesson, as few things in life are clearly right or wrong.

All the qualities that have been traditionally and erroneously applied to competition actually apply better to cooperation. Cooperation builds character, is basic to human nature, and makes learning more enjoyable and productive.

Some of our best and worst experiences at this school of business [New York University] have been our group projects. The best groups work cooperatively with each other, and bring forth an enjoyable experience, a good product, and lasting friendships. The ineffective groups are those that have intragroup competition.

To a great extent, our classes at this school of business [N.Y.U.] have focused on grades to the exclusion of enjoyable learning. Your class has allowed us to question and explore creative ideas and theories in an atmosphere that is devoid of competition, is thus relaxed and conducive to learning. We thank you.

3. Another letter. Fear followed by victory.

My daughter carried back and forth for a month Deming's paper "On Probability as a Basis for Action" (*The American Statistician,* vol. 29, no. 4, 1975, pp. 146–152), afraid to hand it to her teacher of statistics. She finally grew brave enough to hand it to him. He explained to the students at the end of the semester that what he had taught them was no use. They must understand that inference from data is prediction; that there is no assignable probability to being right or wrong in the prediction, that standard errors and tests of significance do not address the problem.

4. Don't beat your children for low grades. The *Washington Post* for 16 November 1990 told us that 110,000 children in Baltimore carried home with their report cards a printed plea from the School Board to parents not to abuse their children for low grades.

Baltimore officials said that they have no statistics on report-card violence. But Peggy Mainor, a child-abuse prosecutor and member of the city's advisory Commission for Children and Youth, said the increase in abuse cases reported immediately after grades are issued has been "enough to catch our notice."

7

The Red Beads

Do not confuse coincidence with cause and effect.—
Gipsie Ranney.

Aim of this chapter. The aim of this chapter is to teach by an experiment a number of important principles. A summary of the principles learned appears at the end of this chapter.

The experiment with the Red Beads. In the experiment in my lectures I play the role of the foreman. "It takes many months to train a foreman for this work, so I'll act as foreman myself." Volunteers from the audience come forth in response to the advertisement that appears further on (p. 156).

Material required:

4000 wooden beads, about 3 mm in diameter:
  800 red
3200 white

A paddle with 50 holes or depressions that will scoop up 50 beads (the prescribed work load).

Two plastic rectangular vessels, one to fit into the other (to save space). In my equipment, the beads (in a plastic bag) and the paddle fit into the small vessel; the small vessel fits into a larger vessel. Sizes, in my equipment:

Larger vessel   20 cm × 16 cm × 8 cm
Smaller vessel   19 cm × 13½ cm × 6 cm

The incoming material (mixture of 4000 red and white beads) arrives at the company in the larger vessel.

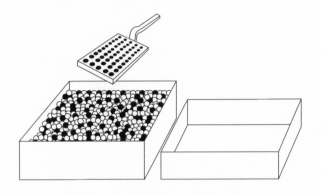

Fig. 17. Beads and paddle.

Procedure

The foreman explains that the company plans expansion to take care of a new customer. The new customer needs white beads; he will not take red beads. Unfortunately, there are red beads in the incoming material (a mixture of white beads and red beads).

Expansion requires that the company hire 10 new employees, so the company advertises:

Vacancies: 10

6 Willing Workers. Must be willing to put forth best efforts. Continuation of jobs is dependent on performance. Educational requirements minimal. Experience in pouring beads is not necessary.

2 Inspectors. Must be able to distinguish red from white; able to count to 20. Experience not necessary.

1 Inspector General. Same qualifications as Inspectors.

1 Recorder. Must write legibly; good in addition and division; must be sharp.

Six Willing Workers come from the audience, step up to the platform, right side.

Volunteers for Inspectors and for the Inspector General come forth. They step up to the platform, stand on the left, the Inspector General between the two Inspectors, No. 1 and No. 2.

A Recorder comes from the audience, steps up on the platform. The foreman explains to her that she is on the payroll, but that there is nothing to do for a while.

The foreman explains that everybody will be on an apprentice program for three days, to learn the job. During apprenticeship they may ask questions. Once we start production, there will be no questions, no remarks; just do your job.

Our procedures are rigid. There will be no departure from procedures, so that there will be no variation in performance.

The Recorder records the names of the Willing Workers, of the Inspectors, and her own name. Her record shows on a form that is projected on to the screen, visible to everybody in the audience.

The foreman explains to the Willing Workers that their jobs depend on their performance. He explains that our procedures for dismissal are very informal. You just step down and collect your pay. There are several hundred people here ready to take your place. There will be no resignation. (The foreman explains that he made this rule because a Willing Worker, in the Salem Inn near Boston, tried to quit when the experiment was about half finished. She had had enough.)

We have work standards here, the foreman explains, 50 beads per day for each Willing Worker. In fact, the only thing that we do right here, the foreman explains to the audience, is that the two inspectors (too many) are independent; they will count red beads independently. Each inspector will record his count on a piece of paper. Neither inspector will see the other's count.

Step 1. Mix the incoming material. Pour the incoming beads into the smaller vessel. Grasp the larger vessel on the broad side, pour from the corner. Merely tilt the larger vessel; do not turn it nor shake it. Let gravity do the work. Do you understand gravity? Gravity is dependable and is cheap.

Next, by the same motions, return the beads from the smaller vessel into the bigger one.

Step 2. Produce beads. Use the paddle, 50 depressions therein. Grasp it on the long side with thumb and finger, insert it into the beads, agitation, no further agitation. Now raise the paddle, axis horizontal, tilt 44°. Every depression will contain a bead.

Step 3. Inspection. Carry your work to Inspector No. 1. He will record on a paper, in silence, his count of the red beads. Then to Inspector No. 2, same for him. The Inspector General compares the counts of the two inspectors. If they disagree, there may be a mistake. If they agree, there may be a mistake. The Inspector General is responsible for the count. He will, when satisfied, announce in a loud voice the count, then the word *Dismissed*.

Step 4. Record results. The Recorder, during apprenticeship, makes no record of the count. Once we go into production, she will show on the screen the count of red beads, work load by work load, as announced by the Inspector General. Everybody in the audience will make his own record, and later, plot his own chart.

The foreman calls the attention of the Willing Workers to our slogans and posters (Fig. 18). They will help the Willing Workers.

Results

Day 1. The first day is a disappointment to the foreman (see the chart, Fig. 19, p. 160). He reminds the Willing Workers that their job is to make white beads, not red ones.

Fig. 18. Posters to help the Willing Workers.

He thought that he had made this clear at the outset.

We are on the merit system here. We reward good performance. It is obvious that David, with only 4 red beads, deserves a merit increase in pay. There are the figures right in front of everybody. He is our best worker.

And look at Tim, our worst performer, 14 red beads. We all like him, but we must put him on probation.

The foreman announces that the management have

Record of the number of defective items (red beads) by Willing Worker, per day. Lot size 50, each Willing Worker per day.

Willing Worker	Day						
	1	2	3	4	All 4	5	
Scott	9	11	7	8	35	16	11
Spencer	6	11	11	9	37	8	10
Larry	12	7	5	5	29	6	9
Seri	11	10	13	9	43		
Tim	14	8	9	11	42		
David	4	11	12	12	39		
All 6	56	58	57	54	225	54	60
Cum x̄	9.3	9.5	9.5	9.4	9.4	9.4	XXX

$$\bar{x} = \frac{225}{6 \times 4} = 9.38$$

$$\bar{p} = \frac{225}{6 \times 4 \times 50} = .188$$

$$\begin{matrix}\text{UCL}\\\text{LCL}\end{matrix} = \bar{x} \pm 3\sqrt{\bar{x}(1-\bar{p})}$$

$$= 9.38 \pm 3\sqrt{9.38 \times .812}$$

$$= 9.38 \pm 3\sqrt{9.38} \times .812$$

$$\begin{matrix}17.66 & \longrightarrow & 18\\1.10 & \longrightarrow & 1\end{matrix}$$

Wooden beads Census count, one by one

Total 4000
Red 800
White 3200
Paddle No. 4

The chart at the left is for Nashville, 14 November 1990. The control limits therefor, extended, predict the range of variation to be expected in the future. The present experiment is an example of the future. For Nashville,

Interpretation of chart

The process exhibits good statistical control. This conclusion is based on intimate knowledge of the procedures prescribed and followed by the six Willing Workers, as well as on study of the chart. This is an example of a constant-cause system. There is no evidence that one Willing Worker will in the future be better than any other. Differences between Willing Workers and between days are attributable to variation inherent in the system (common causes).

The Willing Workers have put into the job all that they have to offer.
One way to decrease the proportion red in the product is to reduce the proportion of red beads in the incoming material (management's responsibility).

The control limits may be extended into the future as prediction of the limits of variation to expect from continuation of the same process.

Inspectors: Frank, David   Recorder: Mary Di   Inspector General: Mark

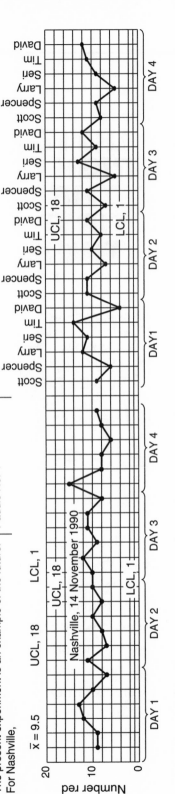

Fig. 19. Data produced by the experiment (Quality Enhancement Seminars, Newport Beach, 16 January 1991); calculation of the control limits; results plotted on the chart (right side); interpretation of the chart. Comparison with a previous experiment (left side of chart) in Nashville, 14 November 1990.

declared a numerical goal—not more than three red beads in a work load.

Day 2. The second day is another disappointment, worse than the day before. The management are watching the figures. Costs are overrunning revenues. I explained at the outset that your jobs are dependent on your own performance. Your performance has been deplorable. Look at the figures. If David can make only 4 red beads on Day 1, anybody can.

The foreman is perplexed. Our procedures are rigid. Why should there be variation?

Look at David. That merit raise in pay, that raise that we gave him yesterday, obviously went to his head. He became careless, and made 11 red beads the second day.

It is obvious that Larry began to pay attention to business, 7 red beads, down from 12 the first day. He has earned this day a merit increase in pay, our best worker.

Day 3.   Posters and bulletins announce that the third day will be a Zero Defect Day. Much fanfare: hire a band, raise the national flag alongside the company's flag; a wine and cheese party the evening before.

The foreman is disappointed and desperate. The Zero Defect Day shows no improvement.

The foreman reminds the Willing Workers that the management are watching the figures, costs are overrunning revenues. The management has served notice: unless the fourth day shows substantial improvement over previous performance, the management will close the place down. Your jobs are your own responsibility, entirely up to you, as I told you at the outset.

Day 4. The fourth day shows no improvement, more disappointment. But the foreman announces good news. Someone in our management—our own management—came forth with a fantastic plan: keep the place open with the best workers. Think of it! Fantastic, and from our own management. A contribution to management the world over, for all time. You are very proud of our management, I am sure; our own management.

The three best workers are obviously Scott, Spencer, Larry. They will work two shifts every day: we must keep up production. The other three may pick up their pay. They did their best. We are all indebted to them.

Day 5. The fifth day begins. The foreman is disappointed with the results. So is the management. The foreman announces that the management have decided to close the place down after all. The wonderful idea to keep the place open with the best workers did not produce the results expected.

Best workers? What was wrong with the wonderful idea to keep the place open with the best workers? What the management meant (implicitly) was best in the future.

Three workers (Scott, Spencer, Larry) were the best in the past. They won the game, past tense. When retained on the job, they turned out to be a disappointment, blasted management's hopes. They had no more chance to do better in the future than any other three workers. It was inevitable that three of the six Willing Workers would be the top three. The three best workers in the past had no more chance than any other three to do well in the future.

Management is not playing games; management is prediction (so stated in 1987 by Dr. Michael Tveite).

Thoughts from a Willing Worker named Ann. A Willing Worker named Ann, after the experiment on the Red Beads came to a close, expressed to me some provocative thoughts. Please put these thoughts into writing, I pleaded with her. Please write them just as you told them to me. She did. Here is her letter.

> When I was a Willing Worker on the Red Beads, I learned more than statistical theory. I knew that the system would not allow me to meet the goal, but I still felt that I could. I wished to. I tried so hard. I felt responsibility: others dependent on me. My logic and emotions conflicted, and I was frustrated. Logic said that there was no way to succeed. Emotion said that I could by trying.
>
> After it was over, I thought about my own work situation. How often are people in a situation that they can not govern, but wish to do their best? And people do their best. And after a while, what happens to their drive, their care, their desire?

For some, they become turned off, tuned out. Fortunately, there are many that only need the opportunity and methods to contribute with.

What do you mean by the same conditions? A good question for advancement of understanding of a process could be this one: What do you mean by continuation of the same process? Answers:

> Same beads. Change beads: the results will be different.
>
> Same paddle. Change the paddle: the results will be different.
>
> Same procedures. This could only mean the same foreman. A change in foreman could produce vastly different results.

In regard to change of paddle, we may look at the figures. I have used over the years four paddles; call them 1, 2, 3, 4, with results in the table below, $\bar{x}$ being the cumulated average over a long series of experiments. New beads came into use with paddles 2, 3, 4.

Paddle	$\bar{x}$
1	11.3
2	9.6
3	9.2
4	9.4

Paddle No. 1 was made of aluminum in 1942 by a friend in RCA, Camden. I used it in the United States. I taught the Japanese with it. Paddle No. 2 was smaller and easier than No. 1 to carry, made for me by Mr. Bill Boller of Hewlett-Packard. No. 3 was made of apple wood, beautiful, but a bit bulky. No. 4 was made for me of white nylon by AT&T Technologies in Reading.

The differences are large. For example, if anyone were paying for 9.2 per cent ash in his coal, and getting 9.6 per cent, he would wonder what is the trouble with the bottom line.

No one could predict what $\bar{x}$ will cumulate to for any given paddle.

Cumulated distribution of red beads. Figure 20 shows the distribution of red beads over 53 experiments, compiled by my secretary Cecelia S. Kilian, as of 11 June 1992. In one experiment there were 20 red beads, 1 bead beyond the upper control limit in that experiment. In my judgment, based on intimate knowledge of the process, I would say that this event was a false signal, not indication of a special cause.

Another lesson from the Red Beads. Knowledge of the proportion red in the incoming material is not a basis for prediction of the proportion red in the output. The work loads produced by the Willing Workers were not drawn by random numbers from the supply. They were drawn by mechanical sampling.

165

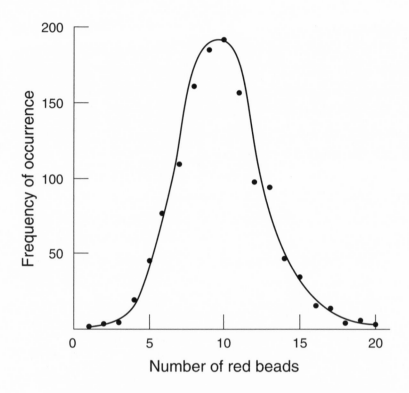

Fig. 20. Distribution of red beads over 53 experiments, up to 11 June 1992.

Japanese engineers, having taken my eight-day seminar in 1950 and 1951, began to wonder about the prevailing method for getting samples of iron ore from a shipload of iron ore. The samples of iron ore are handed to a chemist who performs an assay to estimate the proportion of iron in the ore. The problem is, how much is the shipload of iron ore worth?

The prevailing method of collecting the primary samples was to scoop up from the top of the load a few shovelfuls of iron ore. A committee of JUSE (Union of Japanese Science and Engineering) on the sampling of bulk materials, Dr. Kaoru Ishikawa, chairman, seeing that the average proportion in the output of red beads was not the proportion red in the incoming material, began to enquire into the sampling of iron ore, coal, copper ore, and other materials imported into Japan. The committee went to work on the problem. The table on page 168 shows some results. Note the date, five years after my first teaching of engineers in the summer of 1950.

The Japanese engineers had contrived a new method for collection of the primary samples. Halt at random times during the unloading the conveyer belt that conveys the iron ore from ship to furnace, or to the pile. Every particle of iron ore on board has a chance to be in the sample. By the old method, only the iron ore at the top got in.

The reader may prefer the new method, not because it yields less iron ore than the old method, but on engineering grounds. The new method showed 10 per cent less iron for the Dungan Mine, Class A, and for the Samar Mine, Class D; 2 per cent less for the other two ores (all from India). The difference is worth consideration.

The methods of this committee, continually refined, have become international standards for the sampling of bulk materials.

Yawata Steel Company
22 December 1955

Ore	Class	Old	New	Difference
Dungan	A	59.95	55.33	4.62
Larap	B C	56.60 59.25	55.30 58.06	1.30 1.19
Samar	D	55.55	50.42	5.13

Summary of Lessons from the Red Beads

1. The system turned out to be stable. The variation and level of output of the Willing Workers, under continuance of the same system, was predictable. Costs were predictable.

2. All the variation—differences between Willing Workers in the production of red beads, and the variation day to day of any Willing Worker—came entirely from the process itself. There was no evidence that any one worker was better than another.

3. The output (white beads) of the Willing Workers showed statistical control, was stable (see the chart, Fig. 19,

168

p. 160). They had put into the job all that they had to offer. They could, under the circumstances, do no better. (A principle stated by Dr. Joseph M. Juran around 1954.)

4. We learned why it is that the ranking of people, teams, salesmen, plants, divisions, departments, as is done in the merit system or in the appraisal of people, is wrong and demoralizing, as it is actually merely ranking the effect of the process on people.

5. We learned about the futility of pay for performance. The performance of the Willing Workers—so bad it was that they lost their jobs—was governed totally by the process that they worked in.

6. The foreman gave out merit increases in pay, and put people on probation, supposedly as rewards and punishment of performance. Actually, as it turns out, he was rewarding and punishing the performance of the process, not of the Willing Workers.

7. The experiment was a display of bad management. Procedures were rigid. The Willing Workers had no chance to offer suggestions for improvement of output. No wonder the place closed and the Willing Workers lost their jobs.

8. On the job, anyone has an obligation to try to improve the system, and thus to improve his own performance, and everyone else's. The Willing Workers on the Red Beads were victims of the process. They could not, under the rules laid down by the foreman, improve their performance. (Replacement of a red bead with a white one, or a second scoop, was expressly forbidden.)

9. The management fixed in advance, on no basis what-ever, the price of white beads.

10. The inspectors were independent of each other. This is the one thing that was right in the experiment. Agree-ment of the inspectors (with a possible rare exception) indi-cated that we had a system of inspection, dependable. If the inspectors had come to consensus on the count of red beads, we could not assert that we had a system of inspec-tion. We could only assert that they gave us figures.

11. It would have been good had the management worked with the supplier of beads to try to reduce the pro-portion of red beads in the incoming material.

12. Knowledge about the proportion of red beads in the incoming material (20 per cent) would not enable anyone to predict the proportion of red beads in the output. The work loads of the Willing Workers were not random draw-ings. They were an example of mechanical sampling. Mechanical sampling does not tell us the content of the lot that was sampled. (See *Out of the Crisis,* p. 353.) True, the red beads produced, lot after lot, exhibited a random pro-cess, only common or chance causes of variation.

13. There was no basis for management's supposition that the three best Willing Workers of the past would be best in the future. Three Willing Workers won the game, past tense, but this was no indication of relative standing in the future. Management is prediction, not playing games.

14. The foreman himself was a product of the system. That is, he was apparently in line with the management's philosophy. Production of white beads only was handed down to him by his management. His rewards were dependent on the product of his workers.

The reader may perceive Red Beads in his own company and in his own work.

8

Shewhart and Control Charts

A wise man will hold his tongue till he see opportunity: but a babbler and a fool will regard no time.—Ecclesiasticus 20, v.7.

When I went to the Western Electric Company in Chicago in 1925, people there were already talking about Dr. Shewhart at the Bell Telephone Laboratories, 463 West Street in New York. (This was the Hawthorne Plant of Western Electric, 46,000 people employed there at that time, capacity 48,000. A quarter of them were inspectors.) The people there said that they did not understand what Dr. Shewhart was doing, but that he was a great man and was working on their problems. The aim of the Western Electric Company was uniformity, so that a telephone company that bought their product could depend on it. They advertised, "As alike as two telephones."

They were sincere, putting forth best efforts toward uniformity, but unfortunately nearly always making things worse. They were smart enough to realize that they needed help.

The problem found its way to Dr. Shewhart. He perceived that what the men at Western Electric were doing was to attribute to a special cause any unwanted variation,

172

when in many if not most cases what they observed was variation from common causes. Improvement of the process would have been more productive. They were tampering with a stable system, making things worse. Dr. Shewhart gave to the world new perspective in science and management.

It was my good fortune to meet Dr. Shewhart in 1927 and many times thereafter at the Bell Telephone Laboratories in New York; I also spent many evenings at his home in Mountain Lakes, a ride of about an hour from Hoboken on the Lackawanna Railroad.

On arrival that first morning at Western Electric, following directions, I found my way to Mr. Chester M. Coulter on the fifth floor. I was to join a group of about two hundred people working in so-called research and development. The head of the organization was a Dr. H. Rossbacher. My esteem for him has increased year by year. He had respect for theory. In a conversation that I overheard one time, somebody complained to him that the way we were starting off on a new project was too theoretical. His reply was that if we have ever accomplished anything here, it started off with studies that some people complained were too theoretical. He had no use for the word *practical.*

> Mr. Coulter exacted out of me straightaway a promise not to get caught on a stairway when the whistle blows: those women with their high heels would trample me to death, and there would be

no record. I did not get caught, but I saw what he meant. Of the 46,000 people that worked at the Hawthorne plant, I think that 43,000 of them were women.

Common causes and special causes.   Dr. Shewhart invented a new way to think about uniformity and nonuniformity. He saw two kinds of variation—variation from common causes and variation from special causes.[1] Common causes of variation produce points on a control chart that over a long period all fall inside the control limits. Common causes of variation stay the same day to day, lot to lot. A special cause of variation is something special, not part of the system of common causes. It is detected by a point that falls outside the control limits. This in itself was a great contribution to knowledge. Dr. Shewhart also saw the two kinds of mistake described on page 99. We repeat them here for convenience:

> Mistake 1. To react to an outcome as if it came from a special cause, when actually it came from common causes of variation.
>
> Mistake 2. To treat an outcome as if it came from common causes of variation, when actually it came from a special cause.

[1]Dr. Shewhart spoke of chance causes of variation and of assignable causes. I have replaced his words with common causes of variation, and special causes, only for pedagogical reasons.

Losses from the two mistakes. Either mistake causes loss. We can avoid either mistake, but not both. Anyone may set for himself a perfect record from this hour henceforth never to make Mistake 1. Attribute to common causes any undesired result. Nothing could be simpler. But in doing so, he would maximize his loss from Mistake 2. Likewise, anyone may set for himself a perfect record from this hour henceforth never to make Mistake 2. This too would be easy: attribute to a special cause any undesired result. But in doing so, he would maximize his losses from Mistake 1.

Unfortunately, it is impossible to reduce both mistakes to zero. Dr. Shewhart's next contribution was to conclude that the best that we can do is to make Mistake 1 now and then, and Mistake 2 now and then, both preferably rarely, following rules that will over the long run minimize the net economic loss from both mistakes.

To this end, he constructed what he called control charts, and he prescribed rules for calculation of control limits. Plot points. A point outside the control limits is a signal (an operational definition for action) of a special cause (called by Dr. Shewhart an assignable cause), which indicates the need for action—try to identify the special cause, and if it can recur, eliminate it. If all the points fall within the control limits over a long period, assume that the variation is random, common causes only, no special cause present.

The Shewhart control charts do a good job under a wide range of conditions. No one has yet wrought improvement.

Stable system; prediction. When a control chart indicates no special cause present, the process is said to be in statistical control, or stable. The average and limits of variation are predictable with a high degree of belief, over the immediate future. Quality and quantity are predictable. Costs are predictable. "Just in time" begins to take on meaning.

In the state of statistical control, one may attach meaning to the ability of the process to meet specifications. In the absence of statistical control, no prediction is possible. The process is in chaos.

The control chart in Figure 19, page 160, is an example of a process that is in statistical control. Chapter 10 shows more examples of charts. Some charts there show statistical control, some indicate existence of assignable causes of variation.

When a special cause that can recur has not been removed, the process will be unstable. The performance of an unstable process can not be predicted—Brian Joiner, 28 July 1992.

False signals are possible. It is possible that a control chart may fail to indicate existence of a special cause when one is actually present. It may send us scouting to find a special cause when there is none.

It is wrong (misuse of the meaning of a control chart) to suppose that there is some ascertainable probability that either of these false signals will occur. We can only say that the risk to incur either false signal is very small. (Some textbooks on the statistical control of quality lead the reader astray on this point.)

It is a mistake to suppose that the control chart furnishes a test of significance—that a point beyond a control limit is "significant." This supposition is a barricade to understanding. Use of a control chart is a process for achievement of a stable state, the state of statistical control.

Next step. Once statistical control is achieved (no indication over a long period of time of the existence of a special cause), the next step is improvement of the process, provided the economic advantage hoped for will be a good investment, in view of the expected cost of improvement. Improvement may be defined as:

1. Narrower variation.
2. Move the average to the optimum
   level (see p. 225).
3. Both.

The cost of improvement may be trivial; it may be outlandish, not worth the foreseeable economic gains.

Application to the management of people. Textbooks lead readers to suppose that the principles contributed by Dr. Shewhart are control charts on the shop floor. Actually, this application constitutes only a small fraction of the needs of industry, education, and government. (See the table on p. 37.) The most important application of

Shewhart's contribution is in the management of people, as may be obvious from pages of this book.

Specification limits are not control limits. Specification limits are not control limits. Control limits must be calculated from pertinent data. The reader will note that the control limits that we calculated for the Red Beads (Fig. 19, p. 160) came from the record of the number of red beads produced day by day by each of the six Willing Workers.

A process may be in statistical control yet turn out 10 per cent defective—10 out of 100 items outside specifications. In fact, a process could be in statistical control yet turn out 100 per cent defective.

A point outside specifications indicates need for action on an item, such as inspection, to try to separate good from bad. A point outside control limits indicates need for identification of a special cause, and if it can recur, removal thereof.

My point is that there is no logical connexion between control limits and specifications. Control limits, once we have achieved a fair state of statistical control, tell us what the process is, and what it will do tomorrow. The control chart is the process talking to us.[2]

[2]Eloquently stated thus by Irving Burr in *Engineering Statistics and Quality Control* (McGraw-Hill, 1953).

Examples of Costly Misunderstanding[3]

Example 1. *Question.* Please elaborate on the difference between conformance to specifications and statistical process control. My management feels that conformance to specifications is enough.

Answer. Conformance to specifications may be achieved in several ways:

1. By careful inspection, sorting the bad from the good. Dependence on inspection is hazardous and costly.
2. By work on the production process to shrink variation about the nominal value.

Moreover, there is no way to predict what will happen unless the process is in statistical control. Until special causes have been identified and eliminated (at least all that have appeared so far), one dare not predict what the process will produce the next hour.

The aim in production should be not just to get statistical control, but to shrink variation about the nominal value. It is not enough to meet specifications.

Specification limits are not action limits. In fact, severe losses occur when a process is continually adjusted one way and then the other to meet specifications.

Where are your figures for the losses caused by the supposition made by your management? How could they know?

[3]Examples 1–4 come from my book *Out of the Crisis*, pp. 356ff.

Example 2. *Wrong way.* I watched a man plot a point on a chart. This was in Japan in a factory that made selenium drums. The chart showed an upper control limit; lower control limit zero. I enquired if he would show me how he calculated the upper limit. Answer: "We do not calculate limits here; we just put the line where we think it ought to be."

What was wrong? He was causing loss either from Mistake 1 oftener than necessary, or from Mistake 2. Which one no one could know.

> I mentioned this event in a seminar in Palo Alto. Miss Barbara Kimball of the Cutter Laboratories remarked that "some books tell us to do that." "Please, Barbara," I responded, "surely not: you misunderstand the author: at least I hope so." She showed me; she had a book in hand with this advice. During the next three weeks she sent to me three more books with the same advice. Two of the authors were, so I thought, friends. It may be wise to declare my position on this matter. There is such a thing as guilt by association.
>
> The beginner is entitled to a master for a teacher. A hack can do incredible damage.

Example 3. *The same fault.* Came this letter:

> We reorganized and hired a consultant (a hack, he turned out to be) to teach and train through formal instruction and floor application the prin-

ciples of effective supervision. We combined numerous jobs in both our salaried and hourly ranks. All standards were eliminated from our production people and we set floor standards based on the maximum speed of the equipment as specified by the manufacturer. When 100 per cent is not achieved, the floor supervisor has to identify reasons for performance less than maximum. Our maintenance, technical, and service personnel work on correcting the identified problems.

The consultant was going about it the wrong way. Using the manufacturer's claim as the lower control limit (action limit) is confusing special causes with common causes, making matters worse, guaranteeing trouble forever.

A wiser procedure would be to get statistical control of the machine, under the circumstances in place. Its performance might turn out to be 90 per cent of the maximum speed as specified by the manufacturer, or 100 per cent, or 110 per cent. The next step would be continual improvement of the machine and use thereof.

Example 4. *So obvious, so fruitless.* The vice president of a huge concern told me that he has a strict schedule of inspection of final product. To my question about how they use the data came the answer: "The data are in the computer. The computer provides a record and description of every defect found. *Our engineers never stop* till they find the cause of every defect."

Why was it, he wondered, that the level of defective tubes had stayed relatively stable, around 4½ to 5½ per cent, for two years? My answer: The engineers were confusing common causes with special causes. Every fault was to them a special cause, to track down, discover, and eliminate (Mistake 1, p. 174). They were trying to find the causes of ups and downs in a stable system, making things worse, defeating their purpose.

Flow diagram for use of a control chart. Figure 21 shows steps in the start of a control chart, and its use. It is the responsibility of management to decide when and where to use a control chart. It is the responsibility of engineers and the people on the job to collect data, construct the chart, and work on special causes when they are found as indicated by a point out of control (Fig. 21). Once statistical control is achieved, it is up to management to decide whether to work on common causes aimed at improvement of the process (see right-hand side of Fig. 21).

Accidents. There are two kinds of accidents. The distinction lies in the type of cause.

> Type 1. The outcome (unfortunate event, or extra pleasing event) came from common causes of variation.
>
> Type 2. It came from some special cause.

Why is the distinction important? The answer is that without this distinction efforts aimed at reduction of unfor-

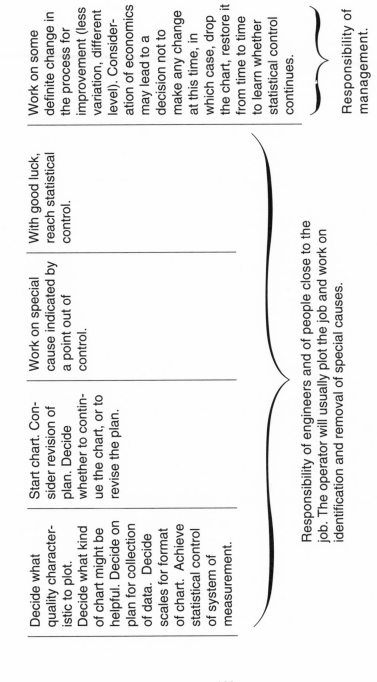

Decide what quality characteristic to plot. Decide what kind of chart might be helpful. Decide on plan for collection of data. Decide scales for format of chart. Achieve statistical control of system of measurement.

Start chart. Consider revision of plan. Decide whether to continue the chart, or to revise the plan.

Work on special cause indicated by a point out of control.

With good luck, reach statistical control.

Work on some definite change in the process for improvement (less variation, different level). Consideration of economics may lead to a decision not to make any change at this time, in which case, drop the chart, restore it from time to time to learn whether statistical control continues.

Responsibility of management.

Responsibility of engineers and of people close to the job. The operator will usually plot the job and work on identification and removal of special causes.

Fig. 21. Flow diagram for use of a control chart.

tunate events in the future (or efforts aimed at increase in the number of pleasing events) will be a disappointment.

For outcome of Type 1, efforts must be directed at the cause-system (the common causes) that produced the outcome.

For outcome of Type 2, efforts must be directed at identification of the special cause that was responsible for the outcome, and at its removal if it could recur. If we direct our efforts the wrong way, we only make things worse. We could now construct a table that may be helpful.

How many accidents come from divided responsibility, no one knows (p. 140).

EFFECTS OF EFFORTS

Efforts directed	Origin of accident	
	Common Cause	Special Cause
At the cause-system (common causes)	Good	Disappointment
At a special cause	Disappointment	Good

Accidents on the highway. Accidents on the highway arise mostly from common causes, for example, drunk driving. Other common causes of accidents may be mostly:

184

1. Unintelligible road signs
2. Different speeds of vehicles on the same road, anywhere from 30 mph to 65 or even 75

Unintelligible road signs are faults of the system: they guarantee accidents. There is nothing special about an accident that comes from drunk driving. There is nothing special about an accident caused by an unintelligible road sign. (See *Out of the Crisis*, Ch. 17.)

More on accidents. Posted in the work rooms of a hotel:

This division has worked
7 days without an accident.

(Day after day, the sign stayed the same, 7 days.)

Also:
Accidents are avoidable.

Another:
Your safety is your own responsibility.

Is it? Mr. Heero Hacquebord, consultant, wished to read a gauge. The steps that he ascended to read the gauge turned out to be rickety, treacherous. He thought that he would tumble off and go sprawling on to the floor. Was his safety his own responsibility? (Taken from *Out of the Crisis*, p. 316.)

Wrong approach. An inspector, on his weekly inspection, complained that there were seven vessels in the plant this morning that contained toxic material, not so marked—no warning. Who was responsible, vessel by vessel, for this failure? Find him; reprimand him, so that this failure will not happen again.

I asked for the figures, week by week, for the last six months. I plotted them. A stable system. The inspector, determined to point his fingers at the people responsible if he could find them, though he did not know it, could only make things worse—more vessels than ever would contain toxic material, unmarked. Fewer unmarked vessels must come from understanding and improvement of the process that produces unmarked vessels. A flow diagram would help.

Fires. The best way to fight fires would be not to have any fires. This would be an impossible numerical goal, so we might settle for something less, namely, reduction in the number of fires. Fire departments could improve their efficiency by learning whether the number of fires per week in a city or in some section of the city follows a stable system or an unstable system. Not every fire comes from a special cause. Let us look at an example.

The president of a company received a letter from his insurance company which stated that unless there be drastic reduction in the frequency of fires in this company's premises during the next few months, the insurance company would cancel the insurance.

The president of the company, naturally worried, sent a letter to every one of the 8500 employees of the company to plead with them not to set so many fires; we may lose our fire insurance. He treated his worries as if the people in the building were the source of the problem.

I obtained the data; plotted the chart in Figure 22. On the assumption that the fires follow a Poisson distribution, with an average of 1.2 fires per month, the upper control limit calculated from the data would be five fires per month. No point lies above the upper control limit.

Had someone in the insurance company, with knowledge of variation, plotted Figure 22, that letter would never have been written. He would have observed that the system of fires is stable, and that the insurance company has a good basis for the rate to set for protection of these premises, and to come off with some profit.

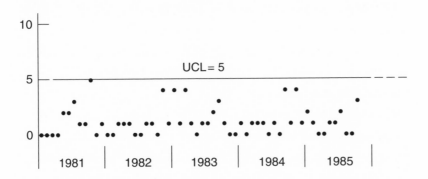

Fig. 22. Plot of the number of fires per month in a business establishment.

One could predict with of course some risk of being wrong, that the same system of fires will continue until the management takes action on the process to reduce the number of fires per month.

Reduction in the number of fires in the future might possibly be accomplished by studying the process that produces the fires in this company. This is totally different from treating each fire as an accident, something special. Certainly we need to put out a fire, no matter what be the cause, but our aim should be to reduce the number of fires in the future. To go about reduction of fires, treating every fire as if it arose from a special cause, an accident, is totally different from regarding it as a product of a stable process. This supposition that every fire is an accident may well block the road to reduction in the number of fires.

Other examples. Does absenteeism in a company exhibit the characteristics of a stable process? If so, only action by management can reduce it. Is any division or group of the company outside the system of absenteeism, a special cause, requiring separate study?

How about the time of transit for deliveries to you, or to your customers? Is it stable, or afflicted with special causes of delays? If stable, how can the time of transit be reduced?

How about accidents on the job? Is their variation stable? Do the data indicate that the accidents come from a stable process? Did any of them come from a special cause?

A word on malpractice. Every suit for malpractice in medicine, or in engineering or accounting, implicates the event to a special cause—somebody was at fault. Study with the aid of a bit of knowledge about variation may lead to a different conclusion: the event could well have come from the process itself—well established methods.

9

The Funnel

It is much better to reprove, than to be angry secretly; and he that confesseth his fault shall be preserved from hurt.— Ecclesiasticus 20, v.2.

Aim of this chapter. The aim of this chapter is to demonstrate by theory the losses that are caused by tampering—management by results (Ch. 2). Anyone may carry out the experiment with the funnel. The only materials required are on hand in almost any household kitchen.

Material required:

A funnel. A funnel in your kitchen will be good. This is not a laboratory experiment.

A marble that will drop through the funnel with a bit of clearance.

A table, preferably with a cloth on it, on which to mark the target and the spot where the marble comes to rest.

Procedure. Place a dot on the tablecloth to indicate the target.

Rule 1. Aim the funnel at the target. Keep it so aimed. Drop the marble through the funnel 50 times. Mark at each drop the spot where the marble comes to rest.

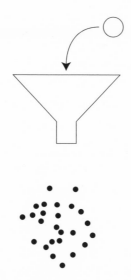

Fig. 23. Record of drops of the marble through the funnel under Rule 1.

The results of Rule 1 are a disappointment (Fig. 23). We get a rough circle, far bigger than we had expected. We aimed the funnel at the target at every drop of the marble, but the marble seems to go anywhere, hither and yon, sometimes close to the target, next drop 30 cm northeast of the target; next drop 15 cm southwest of the target, etc.

Surely we can do better. Why not adjust the funnel at every drop, so that the next drop will come closer to the target? We accordingly construct Rule 2.

Rule 2. At each drop, move the funnel from its last position to compensate for the last error. (For example, if the marble comes to rest 30 cm northeast of the target, move

191

the funnel 30 cm southwest from where it was.)

The results are another disappointment, worse than we got by Rule 1. On the supposition that errors are equally probable in all directions, the variance of the pattern derived from Rule 2 on any diameter through the target will be double the variance of the pattern derived from Rule 1. The expected diameter of the rough circle generated by Rule 2 will therefore be 41 per cent bigger than the diameter of the rough circle generated by Rule 1, and $\sqrt{2} = 1.41$.

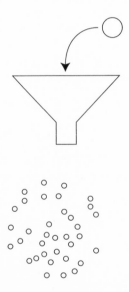

Fig. 24. Record of drops of the marble through the funnel under Rule 2.

Rule 3. Disappointed, we contrive a new rule. Adjust the funnel at every drop, but use the target as the reference point. Set the funnel an equal but opposite distance from the target, to compensate for the last error. Another way to state Rule 3 is this:

1. Set the funnel over the target.
2. Now move the funnel from the target to compensate for the last error. (Contributed by Dr. Gipsie Ranney.)

The results are worse than ever. The successive drops of the marble swing back and forth, with ever-increasing

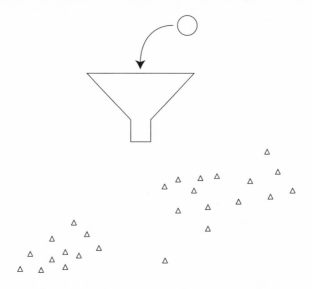

Fig. 25. Record of drops of the marble through the funnel under Rule 3.

amplitude, except that once in a while a few successive drops swing back and forth with decreasing amplitude, only to be followed by resumption of ever-increasing amplitude.

Beaten, we give up the aim to construct a rule that will beat Rule 1, and satisfy ourselves with the aim to achieve uniformity, not necessarily target value. We construct Rule 4.

Rule 4. Set the funnel (after the first drop) right over the last drop (i.e., where the marble came to rest at the last drop).

More disappointment. The marble will eventually move off to the Milky Way.

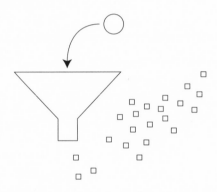

Fig. 26. Record of drops of the marble through the funnel under Rule 4.

Rule 4 was described as follows by Professor William Pietenpol in 1924 at the University of Colorado, when I was one of his students, striving for a master's degree in physics and mathematics.

A man is drunk; knows not which is north, south, east, or west; wishes to go home. He takes a few steps, stumbles, rights himself, takes a few steps, knowing not which is north, south, east, or west; takes a few steps, stumbles, and continues this performance under his handicap. His chance to be within a kilometre of home diminishes with increasing attempts. This conclusion was foretold by Lord Rayleigh in 1898.[1]

Conclusion. Rule 1 is the best of the lot. Our unhappiness with the results of Rule 1 led to formulation of Rules 2, 3, 4, which only produced worse results.

What we ought to have done, instead of formulating Rules 2, 3, 4, was to improve the results of Rule 1. Here are two suggestions:

---

[1]Mathematical solutions are shown in my book *Some Theory of Sampling* (Wiley, 1950; Dover, 1984), pp. 454–466. Reference is made there to Lord Rayleigh's solution in a paper entitled, "On the resultant of a large number of vibrations," *Phil. Mag.,* vol. xlvii, 1899, pp. 246–251; also in his *Theory of Sound,* 2d ed. only (1894), Sec. 42a; and in his *Scientific Papers,* vol. iv, p. 370. The problem of optimum convergency to the target was treated by Frank S. Grubbs, "An optimum procedure for setting machines," *Journal of Quality Technology,* vol. 15, no. 4, October 1983, pp. 155–208. (The problem solved by Dr. Grubbs is not a solution for the funnel.)

1. Lower the funnel. Good. This would decrease the diameter of the rough circle that Rule 1 gave us. Cost? Nothing.
2. Use a fuzzier tablecloth. The marble would not roll so far by any rule. Cost? $11.

Examples of Tampering

Rule 2

Molten copper is extruded through an orifice; comes out hot, mad, sputtering. A man has a job to produce ingots that weigh 326 kg. The weighing of the ingots is automatic. The weight of each ingot appears before him in bold figures. If the weight is below 326 kg, he turns a lever counterclockwise. If the weight is above 326 kg, he turns the lever clockwise.

Uniformity was the aim. Unfortunately, the man's job, though he did not know it to be so, nor did his boss know, was nonuniformity. He was applying Rule 2. He was drawing pay to make things worse. That was his job.

What could he have done that would be better? Simple. Plot points to show the weight of each ingot, one by one. Watch for trends. Watch for level consistently below or above the specification, 326 kg. Still better, plot a control chart, one for $\bar{x}$, one for R, the range, for example, with four successive ingots as a subgroup. Compute $\bar{x}$ and R for each subgroup. If a point goes outside control limits, look for a

196

special cause. Try to identify it and remove it if it could recur. Possibly adjust the level of the weights, if the centre of the $\bar{x}$-chart differs markedly from the intended weight. Also, think about the intended weight, does it make sense? This will depend on the intended use of the ingots.

Rule 2

1. Some feedback mechanisms.[2]

2. Adjust the process when a piece goes out of specification.

3. Typical adjustment by operator.

4. Adjust work standards to reflect current output.

5. Legislation, federal and state, tampering with our economy.

6. Adjustments by the Federal Reserve Board.

7. Reaction to a complaint from a customer. (Of course, keep the customer happy at almost any cost.)

8. Reaction of stock market to news (Ch. 10).

9. Reaction to rumor.

10. If the base material for this lot needs 20 per cent more concentrate, change the specification to call for 20 per cent more concentrate.

11. Engineering changes based on the last version of a

[2]William W. Scherkenbach, *The Deming Route,* p. 30.

design without reviewing the original purpose.

12.   Foreman resetting a process at the beginning of his shift based on yesterday's performance.

13.   Changing company policy based on latest attitude survey.

14.   The cheese comes out of the brine too salty. Accordingly, dilute the brine. If the cheese comes out not salty enough, add salt to the brine.

15.   Continual changes in tax laws, each change to try to correct a previous mistake.

16.   Change of health benefits, each change to try to correct a previous mistake.

17.   Price wars. Company C drops drastically the prices of its automobiles. Competitors drop their prices even lower. Company C beats them. The others in turn go still deeper. Where will the war stop? Who wins it? Some customers win. Society loses because the automotive companies have sunk their cash into rebates; nothing left for research and improvement.

A fuzzy example.[3] We had some supplies left over at the end of the month. We accordingly ordered fewer for next month. We take the opposite action if we run short. We do the same with funds: We adjust the budget for any year based on the preceding year.

___

[3] I am indebted to Dr. Barbara Lawton for pointing out that the action described here may not be an example of Rule 2.

Is this an example of Rule 2? It could be. But if a surplus or shortage came from downturn or upturn of economic conditions, the action described could be wrong, or partly wrong. The question is, how much of the surplus or shortage one month came from changes in economic conditions that will continue downward or upward.

Rule 3

1. Nuclear proliferation.

2. Barriers to trade.

3. Illicit drugs. Enforcement improves. Drugs become scarcer. The price goes up. Higher prices stimulate importation of drugs. Enforcement improves. The cycle repeats itself, deeper and deeper. Where will it end? From Harper's Index (*Harper's Magazine*):

> Average value of drugs detected and confiscated for the year:
> | | |
> |---|---|
> | Per agent | $ 124,000 |
> | Per sniffing dog | $3,640,000 |
>
> [Solution: hire more dogs.]

4. A gambler increases his bet to cover losses.

Rule 4

1. Languages. Example: differences between the Romance languages (Italian, French, Spanish, Portuguese) from each other and from the original Latin.

2. History, unwritten, passed down from generation to generation.

3. Get together and share ideas (without outside help).

4. Folklore.

5. Worker training worker in succession.

> How did you learn your job? I asked her. *Answer:* John, Mary, and Amelia, workers on the job, taught me, was her reply. Then she in turn, after a few days on the job, helped to train somebody new. After a few days on the job, the newcomer helps to train another newcomer.
>
> True, he on the job knows more than anybody about it, but worker training worker in succession goes off to the Milky Way. A better way is to entrust the training to some one person, preferably someone that knows the work and is a good teacher.

6. A group of players in an orchestra tune their instruments sequentially, not against the same source.

7. Executives meeting to discuss what to do in this new economic age.

8. Match color to the last batch.

9. Adjustment of time to a meeting based on the last actual starting time.

10. Copy examples. Learn by example with no theory.

11. Hanging wallpaper.

12. Cost of living adjustment (COLA). Wages adjusted to cost of living. Living adjusted to wages.

13. Use the last board cut as a pattern for the next board.

14. Play "telephone" (also called "post office"). Eight or more people sit in a ring. Someone whispers to his neighbor a short message. This neighbor whispers to his neighbor his version of the message, and onward. What happens to the original message when it comes around the circle? Successive distortions.

Some additional notes on tampering. A stable process, one with no indication of a special cause of variation, is said to be, following Shewhart, in statistical control or stable with respect to the quality-characteristic measured. It is a random process. Its behavior in the near future is predictable. Of course, some unforeseen jolt may come along and knock the process out of statistical control. A process that is in statistical control has a definable identity and a definable capability (see *Out of the Crisis,* p. 339).

Suppose that you have brought a process into statistical control. This you have accomplished with effort. You have searched for each special cause one by one when a point went beyond the control limits. Certain patterns of points on a control chart may also indicate a special cause. You have tried, with apparent success, to identify each cause, and to remove it.

Once you reach statistical control, the difficult problem commences—improve the system. Improvement nearly always means reduction of variation (narrower control limits), though it may also require movement of the average (the central line) to a higher or lower level. Improvement of a stable system requires fundamental change in the process. This fundamental change required may be extremely simple. Example: Provide better illumination in a room.

On the other hand, the fundamental change required may be complex or even costly. It may require authorization and effort higher up. Example: develop better understanding between the upper management of the customer and the upper management of a supplier.

If the system is not worth the cost of improvement, it might be wise to direct effort to other systems more in need of attention. We should study with the aid of a loss function the economics of shrinkage of variation.[4]

A process may be stable, yet turn out faulty items and mistakes. To take action on the process in response to production of a faulty item or a mistake is to tamper with the process. The result of tampering is only to increase in the future the production of faulty items and mistakes, and to increase costs—exactly the opposite of what we wish to accomplish.

[4]William W. Scherkenbach, *The Deming Route,* pp. 42ff.

In the experiment with the Red Beads, were we to halt the line and try to discover what happened on appearance of some high or low number of Red Beads, we would be tampering. Gadgets that hold product to specification are only tampering, increasing costs.[5]

One gets powerful leverage on sources of faults and mistakes by tracing the process upstream. Where are the faults coming from? What is their origin?

A special cause may turn out to be one that can not possibly recur. The temperature of the gas burners went high; ruined $50,000 worth of foam rubber. The cause, arrived at by following a chain of clues, was extra good gas (high number of Btus per cubic foot) that came underground from Oklahoma. No action was deemed necessary, because recurrence will not happen for decades. Moreover, there is not much that the customer could do to ensure no recurrence in the future.

On the other hand, a special cause may be one that can recur. If so, steps to forestall recurrence should be taken, unless the cost to do so seems outlandish. If the recurrence is periodic (every Monday at 10 a.m.), clues to the source may be unmistakable. Sporadic recurrence will require detective work.

Illustration.[6] For numerical illustration of the rules of the funnel, we may take the results of the Willing Workers on

[5] William W. Scherkenbach, *The Deming Route,* p. 30.
[6] I am indebted to Dr. Michael Tveite of Minneapolis for the idea to use the Red Beads as Rule 1.

the Red Beads, shown on page 160. We round off the average $\bar{x}$ to 9, the target. Then 9 red beads translates to 0; 11 red beads translates to +2; 7 red beads translates to –2. The funnel is aimed at the target by all four rules at the first drop. The results of the first drop are the same for all rules. For Rule 1, the funnel (F) is aimed at the target at every drop. We may thus construct the table that follows.

Drop	Rule 1		Rule 2		Rule 3		Rule 4	
	F	Result	F	Result	F	Result	F	Result
1	0	0	0	0	0	0	0	0
2	0	–3	0	–3	0	–3	0	–3
3	0	3	3	6	3	6	–3	0
4	0	2	–3	–1	–6	–4	0	2
5	0	5	–2	3	4	9	2	7
6	0	–5	–5	–10	–9	–14	7	2
7	0	2	5	7	14	16	2	4
8	0	2	–2	0	–16	–14	4	6
9	0	–2	–2	–4	14	12	6	4
10	0	1	2	3	–12	–11	4	5
11	0	–1	–1	–2	11	10	5	4
12	0	2	1	3	–10	–8	4	6
13	0	-2	–2	-4	8	6	6	4
14	0	2	2	4	–6	–4	4	6
15	0	–4	–2	–6	4	0	6	2
16	0	4	4	8	0	4	2	6
17	0	0	–4	–4	–4	–4	6	6
18	0	3	0	3	4	7	6	9
19	0	–1	–3	–4	–7	–8	9	8
20	0	0	1	1	8	8	8	8
21	0	–4	0	–4	–8	–12	8	4
22	0	0	4	4	12	12	4	4
23	0	2	0	2	–12	–10	4	6
24	0	3	–2	1	10	13	6	9

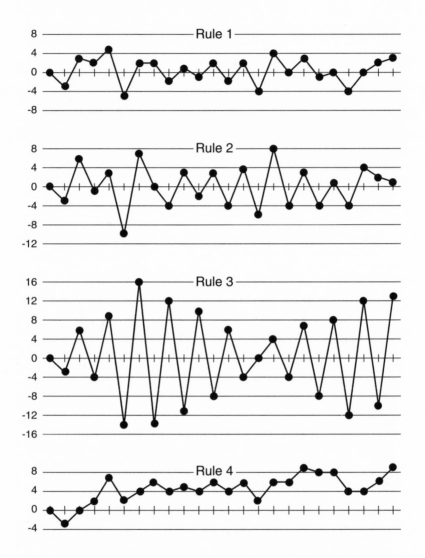

Fig. 27. Illustrations of the rules of the funnel by use of data from the Red Beads (Ch. 7) for Rule 1, target taken as 9. (The data are from the "Result" column for each rule in the preceding table.)

10

Some Lessons in Variation

Prefer a slip on the pavement over a slip of the tongue.—
Ecclesiasticus 20, v.18.

Aim of this chapter. The aim here is to introduce the reader to some easy lessons in variation. Variation is life; or life is variation. No two people are alike. Arrival of a train or of an aeroplane varies from day to day. Time en route to work varies day to day, no matter what be the mode of transport. Anyone that has made measurements in a course in physics has seen variation in readings of (e.g.) a galvanometer, as it measures over and over the same resistance. In the year 1920, under Professor Wilbur Hitchcock at the University of Wyoming, each student in engineering made 10 cubes of neat cement, 10 of cement 2:1, and 10 of cement 4:1. We put them under water to give the cement the best chance to harden. Three weeks later every student measured the crushing strength of all 30 blocks. The tests on all 10 blocks of neat cement were different. Those made of cement 2:1 were all different; likewise those that were 4:1. How could that be? I made them myself, all alike. We learned about variation and we learned a measure of variation, namely, the so-called probable error of each batch.

We saw on page 98 the need for a teacher to understand variation. We have encountered here and there talk of

207

common causes of variation and of special causes of variation. We saw only common causes of variation in the Red Beads (Ch. 7). We have learned that it is important, in the management of people, to understand the distinction between common causes of variation, and special causes (Ch. 6).

Anecdote. The layman, however well educated but not learned in statistical theory, attributes every event to a special cause, unaware of the distinction between common causes of variation and special causes. An actuary at the Metropolitan Life Insurance Company in New York was predictably 12 to 17 minutes late every morning. He would on arrival gather everyone around him to explain how it happened, why he was late this morning. Every morning was to him a new morning, never ever a morning like this morning. It never occurred to him that (except for an accident or a storm) he was dealing with common causes of variation. It never occurred to him to leave home 20 minutes earlier, to let common causes of variation do their work, and arrive on time. But maybe his life would have been dull if he had arranged it to arrive on time: there would have been no story to tell every morning.

Patrick, 11, and the school bus. Dr. Thomas W. Nolan came one day to talk with me; brought with him a chart that his boy Patrick had made, then at age 11. Figure 28 shows my own reconstruction of his chart. Patrick had kept a record day by day of the time of arrival of the bus that came to carry him off to school, and had plotted the points. He recognized by eyeball special causes of delay on two days.

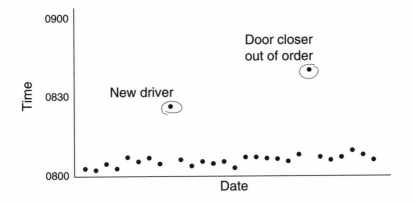

Fig. 28. Time of arrival of school bus, by Patrick Nolan, 11.

Think what a good start in life Patrick had, understanding common causes and special causes of variation at age 11. He had recognized without calculation special causes of delay on two days, and had shown his explanation for the delays.

Is this chart difficult? Patrick mastered it at age 11. This was his science project at school. A good start in life.

Some essential theory of variation could obviously be

taught in the 5th grade. Pupils would come out of school with knowledge in their heads, not merely information.

Harold Hotelling asked how anyone could consider himself in possession of a liberal education without some knowledge about variation.

Allowance, 10 per cent.[1] Engineers in many establishments are allowed deviation of 10 per cent between estimated cost of a project, and actual cost. The 10 per cent comes from stargazing: no basis whatever for it. Figure 29 shows actual deviation, for 20 projects, as percentages from estimated cost. The control limits show that the natural variation of the differences on these 20 projects was 21 per cent above and below estimated costs.

Inventory, computerized. Inventory (how many items on hand) was important to a manufacturer of a product with many styles and colors. A new computerized system had recently been installed to help keep track of inventory. Physical counts were still made after each run of a variety to determine yield. These physical counts were compared with the value in the computerized system. If there was a difference, the value in the computer was adjusted to the physical count.

Although the average difference was close to zero, the first control chart (a) in Figure 30 showed that the difference for

[1] I now draw heavily from a paper by Thomas W. Nolan and Lloyd Provost, "Understanding Variation," *Quality Progress,* May 1990, pp. 73–76.

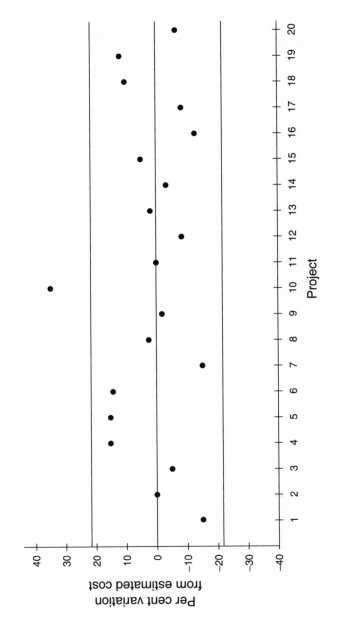

Fig. 29. Control chart for actual costs.

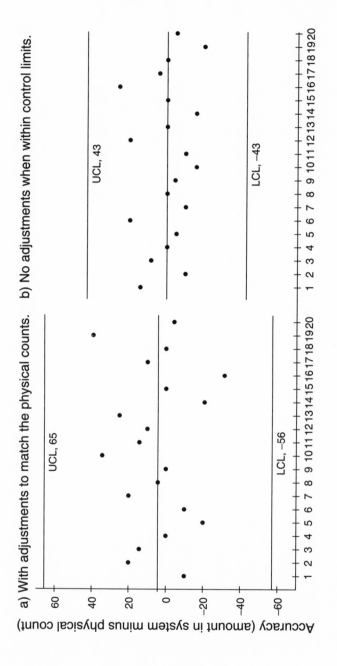

Fig. 30. Control charts for accuracy of inventory.

212

an individual variety of product could be 56 units below zero, or 65 units above. A decision was made to adjust the computer only if the difference between the computer and physical count was greater than 61 units. The second control chart (b) shows the accuracy a month after this policy for adjustments was initiated. The accuracy for individual varieties improved by about 30 per cent. Revised control limits were ± 43 units, which were adopted for adjustment.

Next step, study the common causes of differences, with the aim to reduce further the variation.

Salesmen.   Figure 31 shows graphically the sales of eight salesmen in Philadelphia, each selling two products, Product A and Product B. The manager of sales of a client brought the figures to me. I plotted the chart. Salesman No. 1 is obviously out of line with the others on both products, A and B. Salesman No. 2 is low on Product B but doing well on Product A. The manager of sales was in the mood to replace Salesman No. 1: "He is obviously not doing his job." What is his territory? I asked. Answer: Camden.

Question: How would you like to make a living selling these products to wholesalers and jobbers in Camden? The problem may be Camden, not the salesman. This salesman may have worked harder than any of the other salesmen. He may have worn out more sole-leather than any of the other salesmen, walking around ringing doorbells, trying to sell his wares. He may have made more calls on the telephone than any of the others. The trouble may have been his territory.

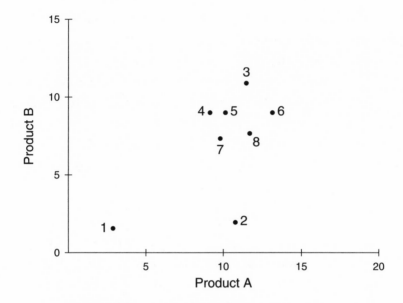

Fig. 31. Sales in percentage (wholesale) achieved by eight salesmen in the Philadelphia area from Product A and Product B. Each point is a salesman.

What should the manager of sales do? If the territory be the problem, a good plan might be to close up business in Camden until the quality of the products of his company improves and his prices come down to the point where a salesman in Camden can match his competition.

Shocks from common causes of variation of trade deficit. Figure 32 shows the trade deficit of the United States over 27 months. The ups and downs are mere manifestations of a stable process. They generate instant shock waves the world over. Of course, there may in the future, and may

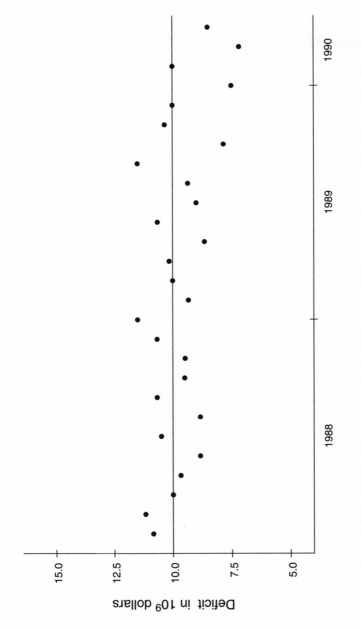

Fig. 32. The United States trade deficit was stable over a long period, though with possibly a slight downward trend.

215

have been in the past, ups and downs that indicate special causes, genuine changes in our economy.

Headlines. The following headlines in newspapers obviously treat the movement month to month as a special cause.

U.S. Trade Deficit Narrows in July Gap Hits Lowest Level in Nearly 4 Years, Surprising Many Analysts

---

Surge in Imports Pushes Trade Deficit Up Sharply

Sept. Trade Deficit at 6-Year Low $7.9 Billion Figure Smaller Than Expected

---

U.S. Trade Deficit Rose in October

One necessary qualification of anyone in management is to stop asking people to explain ups and downs (day to day, month to month, year to year) that come from random variation—Brian Joiner, 28 July 1992.

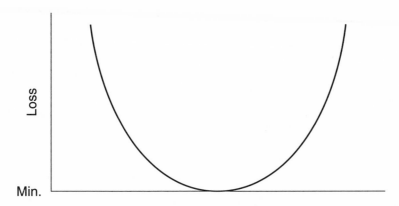

Fig. 33. A loss function.

Note on Use of Loss Functions[2]

Example of a simple loss function. A loss function describes the losses that a system suffers from different values of some adjustable parameter. Use of a loss function is restricted to the realm of losses that are measurable.

The most important use of a loss function is to help us to change from a world of specifications (meet specifications) to continual reduction of variation about the target, through improvement of processes.

An example of a simple loss function might be the output of the people in this room, measured in dollars per hour. The loss function will show dependence of this output on the temperature of the room. Everybody at work in this

---

[2]Shaded areas in this section are not depiction of actual losses. They show sources of loss. For calculation of actual loss, see Henry R. Neave, *The Deming Dimension* (SPC Press, Knoxville, 1990), Ch. 12.

room has his own loss function. For practical purposes, the loss function output against temperature for anybody in this room may be taken as a parabola at the bottom, the temperature at which his output is maximum (Fig. 33). It is easy to show that the loss function for the combination of all the people in this room will also be a parabola. Departure from this optimum temperature will cause loss.

It is important to note that curve and horizontal tangent are for practical purposes coincident over a short range to the right and to the left of the point of tangency. That is, one may move away from the optimum a short distance but suffer only imperceptible loss.

Thus, temperature only two degrees cooler than optimum, or two degrees warmer, would lessen production by only some miniscule amount, too tiny for concern.

But if we move far out from the minimum, there will be substantial loss. Somebody must pay for this loss—Dr. Taguchi called it loss to society (September 1960). We all help to pay for a mistake, a breakdown, failure (bankruptcy) of a company, inept management.

If it were possible to develop a loss function with meaningful figures, one could calculate a sensible amount to spend for air conditioning of the room. How much would it cost to hold the temperature of the room within two degrees of optimum? Within three degrees? Within four degrees? What would be the cost? Where (what range) is the break-even point between loss of production and cost of air conditioning? A crude approximation to the loss function would suffice.

The loss function is usually not symmetrical. It is sometimes very steep on one side or the other, sometimes on both sides. An example is the amount of columbium in sheet steel for easier and more successful welding. A certain amount of columbium in the steel is necessary. Less than the necessary amount is a waste of columbium—no benefit to welding. Columbium in greater amount than the required 3 parts in 100,000 is mostly a waste of columbium—little additional benefit.

An actual loss function appears in my book *Sample Design in Business Research* (Wiley, 1960), page 294. It shows that we only need to come close to optimum allocation of the sample. Very close is as good as best.

Another example. We now make use of the example shown by William W. Scherkenbach on page 30 of his book *The Deming Route* (The George Washington University, Continuing Engineering Education Press, Washington, 1986). Mr. Scherkenbach measured 50 items that were produced with the aid of a gadget that was guaranteed to hold parts within specifications. The gadget performed according to promises, producing the idealized distribution shown as ON (Fig. 34). Mr. Scherkenbach turned the gadget off for another 50 pieces, which gave the idealized distribution shown as OFF. Any reasonable loss function would tell us that the loss with the gadget on is far greater than the loss with the gadget off. In other words, the gadget performed according to promises, but at maximum cost. It would be far better to turn the gadget off.

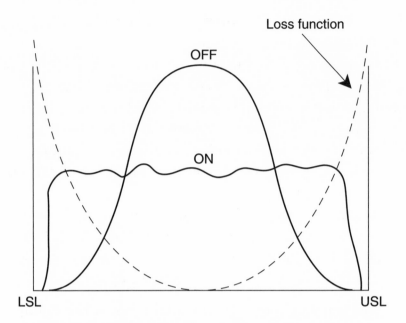

Fig. 34. Mr. Scherkenbach's example. Gadget on, and gadget off. The loss is obviously much less with the gadget off than with it on.

This example is not condemnation of gadgets. It tells us that we need to know what the gadget does. We may be thankful for guidance of the loss function.

It should be noted that the loss function need not be exact. In fact, there is no such thing as an exact loss function. Costs are predictions, rough and crude but they will serve the purpose.

Meet specifications. We are now in position to understand the possible loss from satisfaction merely to meet

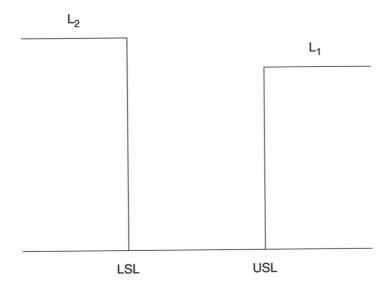

Fig. 35. Here, the loss function is discontinuous. There is no loss so long as we meet the specifications. Loss jumps suddenly at failure to meet the specifications, L_1 if too large, L_2 if too small.

specifications, zero defects. In this circumstance, the loss function is like the one in Figure 35, straight up and down at both specifications, no loss between upper and lower specifications. Test by use of a no-go gauge is an example of satisfaction to meet specifications. We shall soon learn that satisfaction to meet specifications may lead to heavy loss.

Meeting a deadline. Meanwhile, we detour into another example, meet specifications, catch a train, or an aeroplane. Our time is worth something, m dollars per minute. This will be the slope (negative) of the line of loss (loss function) on the left (Fig. 36). Arrival on the platform one minute ahead of departure costs us *m* dollars for loss of time; two minutes ahead would cost us 2*m* dollars, etc. On the other hand, if we miss the train, our loss is L dollars. To miss it by half a minute incurs the same loss as to miss it by five minutes. Hence the loss function jumps straight up from 0 to L, as in Figure 36.

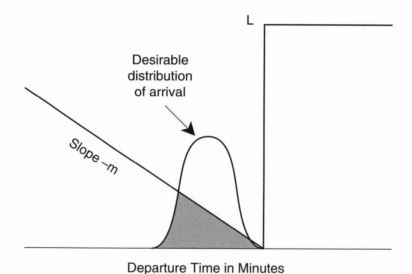

Fig. 36. A possible loss function for failure to meet a deadline, such as to catch a train or an aeroplane. We incur loss L if we miss it.

As a recurring event, catching the train every day, we attempt to create a distribution of time of arrival, centred so that the far tail (3-sigma limit) is just short of the time of departure. In other words, we make use of our knowledge of variation. Our average loss per day will now be the shaded area under the loss function.

> One could complicate the problem by observing that the departure of the train also varies from day to day. There will be a distribution of time of departure. Its 3-sigma limit might be eight seconds, as in Japan. It might be half an hour. Pursuit of this complication would add nothing to our understanding and use of a loss function, so we drop it here.

A stupid illustration is my own problem to park my car to attend church Sundays, to commence at 11:15. There are spaces on church property for 50 automobiles. The spaces are all filled till about 10:50, their drivers still drinking coffee in the Parish Hall after the previous service. Once they depart, the spaces will be filled in a flash by a long line of cars waiting. If mine is to be one of them, I must be on hand early enough. He that arrives too late will not get a space here: he must try to find a space on the street, and there is none. It is better to arrive early, accepting the loss of time to do so, and get a space in the lot, than to arrive a minute late and suffer total defeat.

The theory that we are learning here applies equally well to a deadline. Someone depends on me for work to be completed on or before a prescribed date. Failure to meet the deadline will hold up or derail a project. To meet the deadline, I make an outline of content and steps. A range of dates or of hours would be better than rigidity, to allow for variation in the time required for any step. A plan that allows some leeway not only provides some peace of mind, but would permit review and last-minute revisions, which might well enhance greatly the value of the project.

Advantage of nominal value. We are ready to formalize our oft-repeated advice not to be overcome with satisfaction merely to meet specifications. What else may we do? We must take account of our output, $P(x)$, characterized by μ and σ in Fig. 37. Is our output in the best spot for minimum loss? For the loss-function, we take $L(x) = ax^2$ (parabola), wherein $x = 0$ at minimum loss. Then the loss from production will be

$$\int_{-\infty}^{\infty} L(x)\, P(x)\, dx = f(\mu, \sigma) \quad \text{(Some function of } \mu \text{ and } \sigma)$$

Clearly, this loss goes to a minimum at $\mu = 0$. Moral, strive to move production to the nominal value, $\mu = 0$.

None of this is new. We could quote Mr. John Betti who

made the following statement years ago when he was with the Ford Motor Company.[3]

> We in America have worried about specifications. In contrast, the Japanese have worried about uniformity, working for less and less variation about the nominal value.

Moral: A measure of dispersion is by itself not an indication of achievement. Its centre is much more important. Certainly we should strive for narrow dispersion in the production of nearly everything, but this is only a first step. The next step—essential, as we have just learned—is to centre it on the target value.

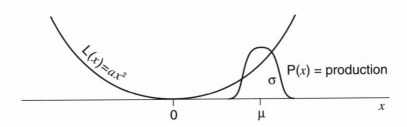

Fig. 37. Moral, for minimum loss strive to move production $P(x)$ to the nominal value where $\mu = 0$.

3 Quoted also on page 49 of my book *Out of the Crisis.*

This simple illustration should put to rest forever use of measures of dispersion like C_{pk}, as it has no meaning in terms of loss. Moreover, it can be decreased to any value merely by widening the specifications.

Conformance to specifications, Zero Defects, Six Sigma Quality, and other nostrums, all miss the point (so stated by Donald J. Wheeler, 1992).

Appendix

Continuing Purchase of Supplies
and Services

Business on price tag? We consider here a number of worlds. Any theorem is true in its own world. But which world are we in? Which of several worlds makes contact with ours? That is the question.

World 1

1. The customer knows what he wants, and can convey to a supplier his needs in terms of specifications or other description.

2. The price paid is the only cost to consider: no other cost is involved.

3. Several suppliers can without question meet the specifications right down the middle, all equal.

4. The only difference between the suppliers is the prices quoted. One is lowest, including transportation and the cost of doing business with him.

5. The customer has no scruples nor prejudice against any of them.

In this world, anyone would be a fool not to do business with the lowest bidder.

We sometimes find ourselves in this kind of world. A homely example is food in a package. Of three grocers handy, one sells it at lowest price. He will get our business.

World 2

1. The customer knows what he wants, and can convey to a supplier his needs in terms of specifications or other description.

2. Several suppliers or jobbers can without question supply the material as specified.

3. They all quote identical prices.

4. One of them, however, provides better service than the others. He has inventory, or has access to inventory. His delivery is dependable. When he says that he will deliver the material this Thursday, he means this Thursday, not just some Thursday. The material will come in the right kind of car, and the car will be clean. He will have a man on the customer's receiving platform to give advice to the customer on how to unload the material, and how to store it, if there be risk of handling damage, risk of warp or of aging from wrong temperature, wrong humidity, wrong way to stack the pieces.

In World 2, the customer will do business with the jobber that provides the best service.[1]

> A possible example is sugar. No one cares what company made the sugar. Sugar is sugar, no matter who made it, no matter who sells it; 998 parts in 1000 are sucrose; the other 2 parts are other kinds of sugar. All six jobbers will quote the same price, the price posted this hour on the Commodities Exchange.

[1] I owe this thought to Mr. James Sherman, at that time manager of purchasing for Kimberly-Clark in Neenah. Mr. Sherman also had only one outbound motor carrier at any one of his 53 platforms over the U.S. and Canada. He expected this one carrier to provide good service; to make good arrangements with an onward carrier beyond the boundaries of this one carrier. Mr. Sherman was willing to pay this carrier enough to provide the service required, and to make a profit doing it.

World 3

1. As in Worlds 1 and 2, the customer knows what he wants, and can convey to a supplier his needs in terms of specifications or other description. However, the customer will listen to advice from a supplier. Some changes in specifications might be worthy of thought.

2. The price paid is not the only cost. There is also the cost of use, predictions of how the material will work in manufacturing, along with consideration of the final quality that will go out the door.

3. Several suppliers tender their proposals, all at different prices, all different in other ways. One or more of them will be concerned about quantities at each delivery, fluctuations of demand, and about the number of days allowed from order to delivery. One or more of the will propose a long-term arrangement, with the aim to follow the customer's use of the material (which might of course be a subassembly) in his various stages of manufacture and onward, with the possibility that small changes from time to time, arrived at the joint effort, might turn out to improve performance and decrease overall costs for the customer.

In World 3, the choice may be difficult. The customer might be wise to divide the business at the outset between two or three suppliers, for further study.

The customer's ultimate aim is continual improvement of quality along with lower costs. Judicious reduction in the number of suppliers with long-term contracts for any one item may seem to offer tempting advantages.

Some remarks. We pause here to recall a few facts of life. Any supplier worthy of consideration possesses specialized knowledge about his products—more than the customer can hope to have, even though the customer will be the user of the supplier's product.

It is good to perceive that customer and suppliers form a system, and that everybody will win on optimization. But cooperation is a two-way street. Can the customer uphold his obligations? The customer has barely enough knowledge to work with one supplier. He will stretch himself too thin to try to work with two suppliers for any one item. Neither of them owes allegiance to the customer. Each of them has his own interests at heart. A customer with several suppliers for any one item is accordingly at a disadvantage.

Another point is that a supplier must be assured of a long-term relationship with the customer in order to make his contribution toward optimization of the system. A one-year contract barely gives the supplier time to get his house in order by the end of the year, at which time the business may go to a competitor.

The idea of several suppliers for any one item, competing with each other for lower prices (as advocated by some authors), makes good talk, but as a practical matter it is only talk, even under long-term contracts. It destroys any possibility of a good relationship between customer and supplier. The losses would be one of those unknowable figures.

Selection of the single supplier. Prime consideration.

Has the potential single supplier sufficient capacity? If not, then he can not entertain any thought of being a single supplier. Two or more suppliers all pushed to capacity is not unusual. I have seen six.

Sudden expansion of a supplier to produce the required volume may turn out to be annoying for both customer and supplier, because of variable quality and uncertain delivery, temporary though these may be.

Sudden jump to a single supplier is inadvisable. There are risks. Go slow. It is not a relationship to enter into lightly. The wise customer will take into account a number of characteristics of a candidate, for example:

His record of past performance.

Capacity and ability to meet demands.

Has his management adopted the new philosophy?

Labor–management relations.

Turnover in management.

How much money does he spend for training? For education?

Turnover on the factory floor.

Has he borrowed money from his pension fund?

What rate of interest does he pay his bank? That is, does his banker consider this supplier to be a good risk?

How about relationships between this supplier and his suppliers? Are they happy, or do they indicate external friction?

Does he depend on inspection for quality? Does he have a system of continual improvement of processes?

Who owns the supplier? If you can not learn who owns him, would you wish to d business with him?

How important is the customer to the supplier? Will the customer provide but a small fraction of the supplier's business?

How important is the supplier to the customer?

An over-riding criterion is the supplier's burning

desire to work with the customer on a long-term relationship backed up by a demonstrable store of specialized knowledge, with management that is trying to adopt the new philosophy.

Advantages of having a single supplier for any one item. A long-term relationship with a single supplier may be a wise decision if customer and supplier play their parts for optimization of the system.

Advantages:
1. Customer and supplier working together for mutual gain and satisfaction.
2. Constant improvement of quality, design, and service.
3. Lower and lower costs.
4. Improved profit for both parties.

Obligations of customer and supplier. There is a strong movement toward the single supplier, maybe too strong. It is feared that many people fail to understand their obligations before they enter into this relationship. The customer has distinct obligations to the single supplier. He must concentrate efforts to cooperate with the supplier to optimize the relationship. It may be a new kind of relationship to both customer and supplier.

Heretofore, under the system of business on price tag, and with several suppliers on short-term contracts (such as a year), competitors watched each other. The single supplier faces a new kind of life; he has no competitor to watch. He is alone with his customer.[2]

The customer has obligation to work with the single supplier,

[2] The sense of this paragraph was pointed out to me in 1986 by Mr. Judson Cordes, then manager of the Oldsmobile engine plant of General Motors in Lansing.

to keep in touch with problems and with help. The days are over when the supplier's obligations end with delivery and acceptance.

It is now common practice for hourly workers of the supplier to see how their product works when somebody tries to use it. What could we do to decrease some of the problems encountered? Conversely, hourly workers of the customer visit the supplier to try to understand his problems, and try to help.

I asked Mr. Ernest Schafer, when he was manager of the Fiero plant, how many suppliers are in your plant any day? About 30. "In olden days, a supplier never came except when we threatened to choke him for poor incoming quality."

It is not an easy matter to receive 30 suppliers in a day, to escort them, introduce them, feed them, treat them with respect.

Some of the usual fears about a single supplier. When he gets a chance, he will choke you, raise his prices. Actually, this has never happened. For sure, a supplier can make an honest mistake in prediction of costs—he can underestimate his costs. Embarrassed, he asks the customer to help him out—either that or he (supplier) may go out of business.

The customer made his choice of supplier. Would he choose a supplier that would choke him if he (supplier) had a chance to do so? Is this the kind of supplier to choose for a life-long relationship of trust and happiness?

What about a catastrophe?—fire, strike, frozen water mains, somebody bought out the supplier and will discontinue this business. The answer is that we can rely on Murphy's laws. There will be trouble. He that hopes for none is living in some other world. Unfortunately, having two suppliers for every item will only ensure twice as many fires in a year, twice as many strikes, twice as many suppliers that discontinue this business. For more trouble, have more suppliers.

What must the customer do when a catastrophe hits his only supplier for an important item? Get on to his motorcycle and on the telephone and find alternate supplies, temporary or forever. It is no joke. It will happen. We can depend on Murphy's laws.

A suggestion offered by Dr. Joyce Orsini is for the customer to ask the sole supplier, in the event of a catastrophe, to make an arrangement with a competitor, to step in and try to provide (unfortunately on short notice) the material or service required.

This makes good sense because the single supplier, if he is good enough to be chosen as single supplier, knows far better than the customer could know his competitors and what they can do. The supplier also knows how a competitor's product will differ from what is currently being supplied.

Engineering changes. What about engineering changes, or other changes that the customer makes? These may raise the supplier's costs.

The supplier may have laid in a heavy inventory of material. The customer has a moral obligation to come through with help to the supplier. The customer should either buy it, or help the supplier to sell it. Trade magazines play a helpful part in disposition of excess inventories.

> A forging company laid in a heavy inventory of a special type of bar steel, only to learn after a few weeks that because the customer will make a change, this bar steel will be excess inventory. The customer should buy it, or help the forging company to sell it. The supplier will call by telephone a number of competitors—maybe one of them is looking for just this kind of bar steel.

Index

Absenteeism, 188

Accidents, 184; two kinds of causes, 182, 184, 188; on the highway, 184

Russell L. ACKOFF, 49, 71

Adversarial competition, 65, 66, 73

Aeroplanes, market for, 4

Agriculture, 5, 61–63

Aim of a system, 49–52, 79

Aims, 41

Air service, 68

Albany, 128, 149

Caroline ALEXANDER, 42

Allowance, 10 per cent, 210

America 2000, 45–48

American movies, 4

American University, 118

Analytic statistical problems, 100, 101

Analyzer, 55

Ann, Willing Worker, 163

Antitrust Division, 74, 75

Archbishop, 107

E. Leonard ARNOFF, 49

Artificial scarcity, 147, 148

Assignable causes of variation, 176

A.S.T.M., 88

AT&T, 75, 76

AT&T Technologies, 165

Nida BACKAITIS, 49, 59, 60, 65, 66, 83, 92

Backtracking, 137

Bad news, 94

Carolyn BAILEY, 51

Edward M. BAKER, 10, 37, 124

Balance of trade, 3

Baltimore schools, 153

Bankers, banking, banks, 32; why did the bank close? 1, 18

Paul BATALDEN, 30

Batavia (Ford), 139

Batteries, 88, 89

Bell Telephone Laboratories, 9, 75, 94, 173

Bereavement, days off for, 129

Best efforts not sufficient, 14, 17, 23

Best workers, 162, 163, 170

Bid, lowest, 34

John B. BIGGERS, 118; Biggers study, 118

Josh BILLINGS, 22

Bill BOLLER, 165

Boston University, 131

Bowling team, 97

Building codes, 90

Irving BURR, 178

Business, school of, what to teach, 143–144

Business, what business are we in? 10

Camden, 214

J. C. CAPT, 120

H. R. CARABELLI, 71

Carburetors, 9, 10

Causes; see Common causes, Special causes

CD player, 135

Cement blocks, 207

Census, Bureau of the, 100, 118, 119, 120

Chance causes of variation, 174

Chanticleer, 102

Child abuse, 153

China, 31

Chi-square, 101

C. West CHURCHMAN, 49

Cincinnati, 113

Civic responsibilities, 149

Clayton Act, 56

Cleveland, 3

Coincidence, versus cause and effect, 36, 154

Wendy COLES, 83, 107

Collective rate making, 77

Columbia University, 68, 144

Columbium, 219

Committee, enlargement of, 107; joint responsibility, 142

Commodities Exchange, 228

Common causes of variation, 33, 174ff., 207, 208, 209; see also Type I outcome

Common sense, beware of, 38

Communication, 29, 106

Competition, failure of adversarial, 65, 66, 73, 121

Competitors working together as a system, 56, 57, 123

Congress, U.S., 27, 76, 118, 119; congressman, 66–67

Constancy of purpose, 24, 51

Control chart, 172, 174–177, 187, 211, 212; flow diagram for,

182, 183; Red Beads, 160

Control limits, 42, 174, 175, 180; contrasted with specification limits, 178

Cooperation and competition, 55, 56, 73, 75, 76, 82, 121, 123, 150–153; between divisions in a company, 71, 82; examples of, 82–87, 88–91; in an orchestra, 96

Copper, molten, 196–197

Copying, danger of, 36

Copying machine, 28

Judson CORDES, 232

Corinthians, 65

Cost, lowest, 34; total, 34

Costs, cutting, 44; of development, 136–138

Chester M. COULTER, 173

C_{pk}, 226

Customer does not invent new product or service, 7

Customers, as part of a system, 142; expectations, 7; happy and loyal, not sufficient, 9

Cutter Laboratories, 180

Data, interpretation of, 100, 103; use of is prediction, 103

Deadline, 221

Debbie, 113

de Beers Consortium, 76

Calvert L. DEDRICK, 119, 120

Defects, zero, not sufficient, 10, 11

Deficit, U.S., 214–216

Delayed effects, 63; of training, 64

Delivery, time of, 79, 80

Demoralization, 122, 144, 148

Destruction of a system, 65–71, 72

Detroit News, 53

Development, to shorten time of, 134–139

Diamonds, 76

Dictionary, 106

Differences, what do they mean? 33

Dispersion, fallacy of measure of, 225–226

Divided responsibility, 140–142

Harold F. DODGE, 94

Dogs, sniffing, 199

Linda DOHERTY, 107, 110

Door closer, 209

Dotted line relationships, 120

Peter DRUCKER, 30, 96

Drugs, illicit, 5, 199

Duluth, 3, 89

Dungan mine, 167, 168

Ecclesiastes, 49

Ecclesiasticus, 170, 190, 207

Education, 6, 8, 45–47, 146, 149

Educational Summit, 48

Electrical components, engine and transmission, 67

Empirical observation, 105

Employment, gainful workers, 117

Engine, electrical components, 67; planning for, 133–135

English language, 149

Enlargement of a committee, 107

Enumerative problems, contrasted with analytic problems, 100

Euclidean geometry, 102

European Community, 76, 91

Experiment with the funnel, 190–196

Experiment with the Red Beads, 26, 27, Ch. 7

Extreme values, theory of, 147

Extrinsic motivation, 108, 109, 122; *see also* Intrinsic motivation

Exxon station, 90

Faber-Castell, 2

Fact, 104, 105

Facts of life, 41

False signal, 165, 176–177

Family environment, 73, 108

Father Bob, 20, 21

Faulty practices, Ch. 2

FAX, 1, 135

Fear invites wrong figures, 94

Federal Emergency Relief Administration, 118

Federal Trade Commission, 24

Fiero plant, 233

Fire insurance, 186, 187

Fires, 186–188

Flat earth, 102

Flow diagram, 19, 20, 57–59, 66, 133, 134, 183; as an organization chart, 60

Foam rubber, 203

Focal length of a lens, 88

Forced distribution of grades, 122, 146, 148

Forces of destruction, 122

Ford Motor Co., 37, 83, 131, 139

Fort Knox, 4

Fourteen points, 51, 93

Lester FRANKEL, 119

Front door, effort required to close, 12

Fuel injector, 9

Funnel, experiment with, Ch. 9

Future, need for planning, 54

Gadgets, 14, 203, 219, 220

Gainful workers, census of, 117

Gallery Furniture Co., 39
Gauge of railways, 89
Bob GEIGER, 129
General Electric Co., 76
General Motors, 109, 115, 232
Geography, 149
Goals, 41, 42, 43–45;
    incompatible, 124; numerical,
    41–44; without methods,
    31–33
Gold stars, 109, 122, 145, 147,
    149
Good news, 94
Government, function of, 123
Grading and ranking in school,
    109, 110, 122, 144–150, 153;
    is a label, 146; is prediction,
    146; produces artificial
    scarcity, 147
Gravity, 42, 157
Great ideas, 117
Greenwich mean time, 88
Grocery store, and lowest price,
    227; shrinkage, 43
Frank S. GRUBBS, 195

Hack, 180
Heero HACQUEBORD, 98, 185
Halifax, 149
Forest HALL, 118
Morris H. HANSEN, 117, 118,
119, 120
Hard work, not sufficient, 14, 17,
    23
Cureton HARRIS, 49, 71
Hatch Act, 61
Philip M. HAUSER, 119, 120
Hawthorne Plant; see Western
    Electric Co.
Fred Z. HERR, 83
Hewlett-Packard, 165
Higher pay, 114
Wilbur HITCHCOCK, 207
Hong Kong, 2
Hopes, 124
Hospital, 22
Harold HOTELLING, 210
House of Bishops, 107
Humiliation, 98, 122, 148, 151
William N. HURWITZ, 120

Ice and water, 101, 124
Illicit drugs, 5, 199
Immunologist, 113
Incentive pay, 28, 39, 122, 144;
    see also Pay for performance
Incompatible hopes, 124
Individual, 130
Inference, statistical, 101
Information is not knowledge,
    104, 106
Ingots of copper, 196–197

Innovation, 9, 108

Inspection, inspectors, 94, 156, 157, 158, 170; dependence on, 179; independent, 170

Inspector General, 156, 158

Integrated circuit, 7, 9

Interactions, management of, 64, 130; between people, teams, 130; *see also* Interdependence

Interdependence, interdependent, 64, 95, 96, 97, 100

Internal Revenue Service, 24

International date line, 88

Interpretation of data, 100, 103

Interstate Commerce Commission, 71–83

Intrinsic motivation, 108, 111, 112, 121, 122; *see also* Extrinsic motivation

Inventory, computerized, 210, 212

Iron ore, 3, 100, 105, 166–168

Kaoru ISHIKAWA, 167

Ivy League universities, 75

Brian L. JOINER, 42, 129, 176, 216

Joint responsibility, 142

John E. JONES, 83

Joy in learning, 109, 121, 123, 145

Joy in work, on the job, 60, 97, 109, 114, 123, 146

Joseph M. JURAN, 169

JUSE (Union of Japanese Science and Engineering), 60, 167

Just in time, 176

Norb KELLER, 109, 115

Cecelia S. KILIAN, 165

Barbara KIMBALL, 180

Kimberley mine, 76

Kimberly-Clark, 228

Robert KLEKAMP, 126

Knowledge, contrasted with information, 104, 106; theory of, 101, 102

Alfie KOHN, 113, 128, 147, 150

Lenore JACOBSON, 26

Japan, 57, 180; made in, 5

Jobber, *see* Supplier

Job description, needs revision, 64–65

Thomas H. JOHNSON, 95

Larap mine, 168

Irving LANGMUIR, 116

Louis LATAIF, 131

William J. LATZKO, 146

Barbara LAWTON, 49, 59, 92, 198

Leaders, leadership, Ch. 5; of change, 116
League, Sacred Heart, 18, 19
Mary LEITNAKER, 106
Lens, focal length, 88
Clarence Irving LEWIS, 101
Libby-Owens-Ford Glass Co., 118
London, moving stairs, 34
London Times, 22
Loser, business with, 72
Loss function, 202, 216ff.
Loss-leader, 97
Loss, sources of, Ch. 2
Lowest bid, 34, 227
Luke, 92

Peggy MAINOR, 153
Malpractice, 188
Man, two meanings, 149
Management, is prediction, 101, 102, 163, 170; not playing games, 163, 170; of interactions, 130; of people, 37, 100, Ch. 6, 177, 178; suggestions for better practice, Ch. 2
Manager, role of a manager of people, 125–128
Marble; *see* Experiment with the funnel

Market share, 56
Marriage, 72; joint responsibility, 142
Mass production, 145
M.B.O. (management by objective), 14, 30–31, 40, 96
M.B.R. (management by results), 14, 31, 33, 46, 144, 190
Jim McINVALE, 39
Measurement as a process, 100, 104
Mechanical sampling, 163, 170
Merit pay, merit rating, merit system, 14, 25–27, 47, 122, 161; demoralizing, 113; for teachers, 146; Red Beads, 159, 161, 169
Mesabi Range, 3
Metro, 34
Michigan Bell Telephone Co., 71
Milky Way, 194, 200
Minneapolis, 149
Mistakes, losses from, 175, 180; two kinds of, 99, 174, 175, 180
Monetary reward (as recognition), 110, 112–114
Monopoly, 73–75; and the Postal Service, 76
Montreal, 149
S. MORIGUTI, 57

Motivate people; *see* Extrinsic motivation, Intrinsic motivation
Motor carriers, 44, 77, 78–83, 228
Murphy's Law, 233, 234

Nashua Tape Co., 128
National Airport, 113
National Cooperative Research Act, 56
Naval bases, 53, 66
Henry R. NEAVE, 83, 217
Negotiation, basis for, 97–98; requires operational definitions, 106
Lloyd S. NELSON, 35, 41, 43
New driver, 209
New engine, planning for, 133, 134
New machinery, 14, 15
New York Times, 95
New York University, 68, 71, 144, 152
No defects, no jobs, 10–12
Patrick NOLAN, school bus, 208, 209
Thomas W. NOLAN, 208, 210
Nominal value, advantages of, 224
No true value; *see* True value

Nuclear power plant, 44
Numerical goals, 31–32, 41–47, 122, 161; in education, 45–47

Obligation of a component, 97
Oklahoma, 203
Olympic games, 147
Open entry, 73
Operational definitions, 106–108
Orchestra, 96, 97, 200
Ore, iron; *see* Iron ore
Organization chart, flow diagram as, 58
Orlando, 69
Joyce ORSINI, 45, 110, 234
Oscilloscope, 55
William OUCHI, 55
Outside view, *see* Profound Knowledge
Overjustification, 110, 112, 113

Paddles, comparison of, 164–165
Palo Alto, 180
Patterns, 201
St. PAUL, 65
Pay for performance, incentive pay, 28–29, 109, 144, 169
Payroll card, 141; problems with, 140–142

PDSA (Plan-Do-Study-Act) cycle, 32, 59, 131–133

People, management of, Ch. 6

Performance and style, 12, 13

Performance, can not be measured, 28, 169; is governed by the system, 169; jobs depend on, 169

J. William PFEIFFER, 83

Philadelphia, 214

William PIETENPOL, 195

Plane Euclidean geometry, 102

Planning for a new engine, 133, 134

Plant, why did it close? 17–18

Poisson distribution, 187

Alfred POLITZ, 1

Popular vote, 107

Postal routes, sample of, 118

Postal Service, U.S., 35, 76, 118

Posters and slogans, 158, 159

Power, sources of, 126

Practical, 173

Prediction, 20, 176; management is, 101, 102; inference from data or experiment, 103, 153

Price, business based on, 227, 230; see also lowest bid

Price fixing, 73–74

Price wars, 198

Prima donna, 72, 96

Prime numbers, 104

Prizes, 149, 150

Production viewed as a system, 57–59

Profit centres, 29, 50, 68, 83

Profound knowledge, system of, 49, Ch. 4; by invitation, 92; comes from the outside, 92, 101; four parts of, 93

Promotion, 143

Lloyd PROVOST, 210

Psychology, 93, 107; entwinement with statistical theory, 93, 94

Purchase of supplies and service, Appendix

Pygmalion effect, 26

Pyramid, 60

Quality, and the consumer, 2; delegation of, 35; responsibility of management for, 15–19; responsibility of operator for, 16; suggestions for improvement, 13–14; trade dependent on, 2, 18; where made? 18; Vice President of, 14, 35

Quebec, 149

Quotas, 32, 38

INDEX

Railway gauge, 89

Rain, 12

Random changes, random forces, random impulses, 107

Random numbers, random sample, 118, 165, 170

Random variation, 168, 216

Ranking (people, teams, divisions), evils of, 25, 38, 94, 108, 113, 144, 145–150, 169

Gipsie RANNEY, 33, 36, 154, 193

Rate bureaus, 77, 78

Rating people; *see* Ranking people

Rational plan, 103

Rational prediction, 102

Lord RAYLEIGH, 195

Bryce REA, 77

Red Beads, experiment with, 26, 27, Ch. 7; lessons, 165, 168–171, 208; Recorder of, 156, 157, 158

Report cards, 153

Reward, 113, 114

Road signs, 185

Rob RODIN, 40

Robert ROSENTHAL, 26

H. ROSSBACHER, 173

Rothamsted, 61

Edward ROTHMAN, 146

Royal Philharmonic Orchestra of London, 96

Rumor, reaction to, 197

Sacred Heart League, 18–21, 59

Safety, 185

St. PAUL, 65

Salary instead of commission, 39

Salem Inn, 157

Salesmen, 28, 39, 213–214; of the month, 38; on salary, 39, 40

Sales territory, 39, 213–214

Samar mine, 167, 168

Same conditions, 164

Sample, random, 118

Sampling, in the Census, 100, 118, 119, 120; mechanical, 165, 170; of bulk materials, 166–168

San Diego, 105

San Francisco, 32

Ernest SCHAFER, 233

Schenectady, 149

William W. SCHERKENBACH, 38, 56, 83, 145, 197, 202, 203, 219, 220

Peter SCHOLTES, 38

School Board, 153

School bus, 208–209

School of business, 144

Schools, system of, 62, 72; *see
also* Education
Scott Paper Co., 71
Scrap metal, 3, 4
Sears Roebuck & Co., 31
Secretary of Education, 45
A. Richard SEEBASS, 61, 62
Selenium drums, 180
Peter M. SENGE, 64
Services, importance of, 6, 145;
purchase of, Appendix
Share of market; *see* Market share
James SHERMAN, 228
Walter A. SHEWHART, 90, 99,
173, 174, 175, 177–178, 201
Shewhart control charts, Ch. 8;
see also Control chart
Shewhart cycle; *see* PDSA cycle
William SHOCKLEY, 9
Short-term thinking, 24–25
Shrinkage, 43
Leslie E. SIMON, 121
Six Sigma Quality, 226
Slogans, *see* Posters and slogans
Sources of power, 126
Special causes of variation, 33, 34,
174, 178, 182ff., 203; *see also*
Assignable causes, Common
causes, Type II outcome
Special help, in need of, 127, 147
Specification limits, not action

limits, 179; not control limits,
178
Specifications, 14, 178, 179, 181,
197, 217, 219, 220, 221, 226,
227, 228, 229
SQC (statistical quality control),
14, 160, Ch. 8
Stable process, stable state, stable
system, 42, 99, 123, 160, 168,
176, 182, 186, 188, 202
Stable system of fires, 187
Stamping out fires, 123
Frederick F. STEPHAN, 119, 120
Stern School of Business, 147
J. Stevens STOCK, 119
Stoichiometric mixture, 10
Samuel A. STOUFFER, 119, 120
Style, 11, 12, 13
Sugar, 228
Suggestions for better
management practices, Ch. 2
Supplier, advantages of single,
232; fears about single, 233;
obligations of customer and,
232–233; problems with
single, 231, 234; selection of
single, 230
Suppliers, and customers as a
system, 142, 230; and
toolmakers, 139; reduction in
number of, 229; selection of,
227–229

Supplies, purchase of, Appendix

System, theory of, Ch. 3; appreciation for, 93, 95, 125; can not understand itself, 54, 92, 101; destruction of, 65–71, 72; improvement of, 33, 125, 127, 169, 177, 202; of schools, 62, 63

Table, wash, 64

Genichi TAGUCHI, 218

Taguchi loss function, 218

Tampering, 66, 173, 190, 196–204

Teachers need to understand variation, 98

Telephone system, 75

Test of hypothesis, 101

Test of significance, futility of, 101, 153; a control chart is not a, 176, 177

Test or experiment, 100, 103

Theory, leads to prediction, 102, 103; need for 102–103; of knowledge, 101, 102; *see also* Knowledge

Lester C. THUROW, 135

Time for development, 134

Time of delivery, 79, 80, 188

Total cost, 34

Toxic material, 185

Trade deficit, 214–216

Trade, necessity for, 2

Traffic lights, 88

Training, benefit not measurable, 20

Transformation, 17, 78, 92–93, 116, 123–124; first step, 92, 93; of the individual, 92, 93; pictorial effect of, 124

Transportation, system of, 77–83

Travel department, 68, 69, 97

Myron TRIBUS, 20, 21

True value (none), 104–105

Yoshi TSURUMI, 27

t-test, 101

Michael TVEITE, 163, 203

Type I outcome, 184

Type II outcome, 184

Unemployment, census of, 118, 119

Union and management, negotiations, 97

Universities, aid to students, 75, 76

Vacuum tubes, 9, 10

Variation 93, 98–100, 160, 168, 177, Ch. 10; knowledge

about, 98; teachers need to understand, 98; two kinds of causes, 174
Vice President in Charge of Quality (wrong way), 14, 35

Washington, 31, 34, 152
Washington Post, 26, 149
Waste; *see* Loss, sources of
Water and ice, 101, 124
John WEBB, 119
Western Electric Co., 172, 173; Hawthorne Plant, 172
Western Union Telegraph Co., 76
Westminster Abbey, 65
What business are we in? 10
Donald J. WHEELER, 226
Where is quality made? 18
John O. WHITNEY, 44
Willing Workers (on the Red Beads), 156ff.
Wind, 12
Winnipeg, 89, 149
Win, win, 29, 149
Work standards (quotas, time standards), 157
Worker training worker, 107, 200
Works Progress Administration, 119

Yawata Steel Company, 168
Kosaku YOSHIDA, 75

Zero Defect Day, 161
Zero defects not sufficient, 11, 12, 14, 16, 226
Zero-sum, 82